AF568143

SELF-HELP GROUPS AND MICRO-CREDIT INSTITUTIONS

Edited by

Dr. Sudhansu Sekhar Nayak
Lecturer
Deptt. of Commerce
R.N. College, Dura
Berhampur, Ganjam
(Orissa)

&

Dr. Anil Kumar Sahu
M.Com., MBA
Professor
Deptt. of Business Administration
Berhampur University
(Orissa)

DISCOVERY PUBLISHING HOUSE PVT. LTD.
NEW DELHI-110 002

Published by:
Tilak Wasan

DISCOVERY PUBLISHING HOUSE PVT. LTD.
4831/24, Prahlad Street, Ansari Road
Darya Ganj, New Delhi-110002 (India)
Phone : +91-11-23279245, 43764432
Fax : +91-11-23253475
E-mail : parul.wasan@gmail.com
discoverypublishinghouse@gmail.com
web : www.discoverypublishinggroup.com

***First Edition:* 2011**
ISBN: 978-81-8356-918-7

Printed at:
Shree Balaji Art Press
Delhi

Preface

Micro-finance programmes envisage increasing out reach of small financial services through Self-help Groups (SHGs) in general and women groups in particular. Since the SHG is a small and informal group of 10 to 20 persons drawn from relatively homogeneous background, the members who join the groups know what benefits they would attain from the group through micro-finance. Micro-finance has to be utilized in such a way that it benefits the SHGs to improve the quality of life of their members and if properly implemented would lead to the increment in income by enhancing member's productivity and ensuring timely repayments and adequate social monitoring. The SHGs need to firm up their financial and economic norms meant for selection of appropriate beneficiary and subsequent disbursement of credit to the needy. Hence, there is a need of implementation of schemes for women empowerment which should reach them in proper manner, so that the women empowerment will fulfil their aims and objects. Hope it will be helpful to the readers, researchers and academicians purposefully.

Dr. S.S. Nayak

Dr. A.K. Sahu

Contents

1

Self-help Groups and Micro-credit Management in Orissa *Accelerators of Women Empowerment*

Dr. Sudhansu Sekhar Nayak*
Dr. Anil Kumar Sahu**

Introduction

Women in India constitute around half (48% as per 2001 Census) of the country's population. Hence, they are regarded as the "Better half of the Society". In the past, women were confined to the four walls of the house performing household chores. They were totally dependent on men for their survival and growth. Hence, they were regarded as '*abla*', i.e. weak and helpless. But, the scenario has changed significantly over the period due to both increasing education and awareness among the women themselves, on the one hand, and ever increasing concern of the Government to empower women, on the other. The

* Sr. Lecturer in Commerce; Ramnarayan College, Dura Berhampur – 10, Ganjam (Orissa)

** Professor in MBA; Deptt. of Business Administration, Berhampur University; Bhanja Bihar – 7 (Orissa) result is women today have treated into almost all spheres of human activities including industry and have been performing exceedingly well making landmarks in their respective fields.

Women Self-help Groups (SHGs) in India have been recognized as an effective instrument for the development and empowerment of women in rural and urban areas to enforce their entitlements to education and health and decent livelihood. The access to credit can be seen as the motivational factor behind the formation of SHGs and the bond that sustain the groups over time. However, SHGs have a potential that goes beyond the management of loan, once a group has been formed the credit link with the bank is established and then the groups meets at regular intervals to take up other economic and social activities. SHGs provide a forum in which the members of the group can discuss various issues and their day to day problems of life.

During the past few years, the SHGs movement has taken a district shape with the support of many government and non-governmental organizations (NGOs). People on a large-scale, specially the socially and economically backward class, have appreciated it were initially promoted by some NGOs in response to the failure of formal banking institutions to reach the poor households. The idea was based on prevalence of informal saving and credit groups. Rotating savings and credit association funds, chit funds, etc. in villages enabled poor people to pool their money and lend it to their members. The innovation of SHGs was in forming groups exclusively of the poor, having small homogeneous groups size and convencial formal banks for lending to SHGs.

With the issue of women's empowerment occupying centre stage in all poverty and development debates, both nationally and internationally, ways and means to make women's access to funds easier gained momentum. In this context, SHGs are fast gaining importance and popularity. The present study is an attempt to evaluate and analyze the status and impact of SHGs in the State of Orissa in India with a special emphasis on economic status of women.

Self-help Groups and Micro-credit Concept

The Self-help Groups is a small economically homogeneous and affinity group of rural poor, generally not exceeding 20 members, voluntarily coming together to save small amounts regularly, to mutually agree to contribute to a common fund, to have collective decision-making, to save conflicts through collective leadership and mutual discussions and provide collateral free loans at terms decided by the group at market driven rates. The Grameen Bank of Bangladesh started in the year 1976 the practice of poor group monitoring to reduce the lending risk was introduced as an alter native to physical collateral. In India, Self-employed Women's Associations (SEWA) which was a trade union for women and, later entered into the field of micro-credit, has grown into the biggest Women's Co-operative Bank in the country.

In South India, the Mysore Resettlement and Development Agency (MYRADA) was the first NGO to introduce Micro-credit in the eighties. A number of approaches have been tried in different parts of the world for implementations of micro-credit programmes, of these, group based approach had shown great success. Tow types of methodologies, which have gained popularity amongst the NGOs in South Asian Region are the Self-help Group Model and the Grameen Bank Model.

In the SHG model, a group of 10 or more homogeneous members are formed. This is followed by six months to two years of regular savings. There is les focus on external loans and mostly it is the internal savings, that are rotated among the members as loans. Once the group show a matured financial behaviour, banks are encouraged to lend to the

SHGs. These loans are usually through direct linkage of the SHGs with the banks. Under some programmes, there is practice to provide grants to new groups in the form of seed capital or matching contributions. The programmes based on the SHGs model shown substantial development impacts, in terms of growth levels in outreach and their financial stability. The simplicity of SHGs approach made them very popular approach in micro credit delivery system in India.

Micro-credit as a vital tool for financially empowering the poor in India and Orissa has evoked considerable interest both from the government and the private sector. Poverty reduction is one of the major goals of development in Orissa, since the advent of planning. To contain poverty, Micro-credit as one development approach can contribute a lot for providing a minimum standard of living for all within a reasonable period. There are two major models under micro-finance i.e. self-help groups-bank linkages and micro-finance institutions. It seems that SHGs are the real grass-root setups for micro-credit growth. In Orissa, 48 per cent people suffer from material deprivation, social deprivation, political deprivation and intellectual deprivation, and the state has poor banking facility, inadequate spread of infrastructure and poor health facilities. There is an urgent need for tiny amounts of loans to people in the least urbanized state of the country, because according to R.B.I., over 40 per cent of Indians and also Orissa do not have bank accounts. The estimates of N.S.S. 59th round (2003) reveal that, only 27 per cent of farmers of the country have received credit from formal sources and 22 per cent from informal sources. The remaining 51 per cent mostly marginal farmers have virtually no access to credit. A more or less similar picture exits in Orissa.

Indian Scenario

The entry of National Bank for Agriculture and Rural Development (NABARD) into this filed in 1990 has changed the scenario drastically among the formal financial institutions. Under the SHG-Bank Linkage Programme Commercial, rural and cooperative banks lend to SHGs and NABARD to refinance these loans at a subsidized interest rate. The banks which were reluctant to the lend to the poor are now supporting in a big way. The success of the SHG programmes is due to the higher repayment rates of over 95 per cent compared to the other poverty lending programmes that had repayment rates less than 50 per cent.

It has been relished that, group approach is relatively more effective and sustainable to initiate and implement development programmes. However, the poor may not be able to form the groups by themselves due to lack of proper education and management skills. Therefore, different kinds of promotional agencies have come forward to function as catalysts and facilitators for these SHG groups. These includes not only the government, NGO, but several professional and development agencies as well. The major role of Self-help Promoting Institutions (SHPIs) is to support and gain SHGs for capacity building and management of Micro enterprises. Such meaningful thrift and credit activities may lead to enhancement to economic stats of these women groups and this help the rural poor women to ensure their livelihood through active participation in SHG activities.

SHG in Orissa

In Orissa Mission, Shakh companies were launched on 8th March, 2001 with an objective to form one lakh women SHGs by March 2005. The target is further enhanced to two lakh WSHG by March 2008. Total number of SHGs formed by the end of March 2006 was 1,90,785 as against the target (40,000 SHGs) at Panchayat, Block, District and State levels.

The foundations are working on assessment of training needs and marketing of SHG products. Hindustan Lever

Ltd. is working as a strong partner in transference marketing still to the WSHG through their branded products under the scheme project SHAKH. So far, 1478 still have been involved in the project by spreading its network to 22 districts of the State.

The State government have given more priority to the WSHGs in implementing the development programmes meant for rural uplift. The WSHGs are involved in kerosene dealership and are content with supply of food to children and mother suffering from malnutrition. It is also involved in the implementation of mid-day-meal programmes, total sanitation campaign and reduction of infant mortality rate (IMR) a total number of 1.60 lakh SHGs have been credit linked by different banks in the State.

An NGO called Biswa commenced its operations in States of Chhattisgarh, Jharkhand, West Bengal, Uttarakhand, Delhi, Andhra Pradesh, and Orissa. The activities of the organization are concentrated in the districts of Sambalpur, Sonepur, Bargarh, Keonjhar and Deogarh districts of Orissa. Biswa strives hard to encourage SHGs to take up production/processing activities, employment generating activities, innovation projects, rejuvenation of a sick unit of district administration, expansion of the customer base for the products and savings members groups from the additional expenses of marketing.

Review of Literature

There have been several studies on the SHG movement and its efficiency as an approach for poverty reduction and enhancing the economic status of women. Many studies suggest that the group method is better for delivering the development status for women. The studies conducted in and outside the country have also reconfirmed that the SHG movement has not only created awareness among women but has also helped them to take up income generating activities, thereby facilitating economic status and empowerment of women. Some of the important studies taken up in different parts of the country during the past decade are reviewed for better understanding and to justify the need for the present study.

Shandilya (1996) points out that the success of any productive venture of SHGs would depend on the availability of appropriate information, markets, and the linkage with banks are extremely helpful for SHGs to undertake income generating activities. The study suggest is that despite constant improvement in the status of women released to the physical quality of life indices, women are still associated with traditional occupations and the situations can be overcome through proper training and support systems.

Karmakar, K.G. (1998) who reviewed SHG programme in Orissa is of the opinion that, the empowerment opportunities through SHGs for women and the chance for them to take up income generating projects and assist them in their family incomes has been a powerful incentive. However, both banks and NGOs react to see this an alternative channel for rural credit delivery systems in Orissa. He suggests that the banks need to explore possibility of linking up more SHGs as part of their legitimate business activity. The operational programme in SHGs bank linkage model need to be sorted out for wider application.

Puhazhendhi, V. (2000) examined the various aspects of the SHGs bank linkage programme, such as characteristic of groups, saving pattern, bending norms, repayment performance, empowerment and sustainability of groups. He suggested that the federal structure of SHGs provide effective support to the groups in coordination, monetary and linkage with banks and other social activities. The NGOs plays a vital role in organizing and monitoring of SHGs in Tamil Nadu.

Singh, O. (2003) examined the experience of MYRADA in fostering SHGs. The vision of MYRADA is building up people's institutions to ensure access and control over resources for sustainable development and self-reliance. It has over 1000 SHGs of women which focus on women's rights and access to control of resources which they require to ensure a sustainable livelihood.

Prasad, Hemalata *et al.* (2004) argues that SHGs need better infrastructure and institutional support for sustaining the groups in view of the increased competition in the economic reforms era. Skill up-gradation in non-farm sector will prepare SHGs for better competition and boost SHGs, the marketing prospects. She pleads that technological intervention is essential for working environment of SHGs and for the SHPIs operating in the field.

Nayak, B. (2005) has evaluated the SHG Bank linkage programme in Kalahandi District of KBK region in Orissa suggests that the NGOs and Mission Shakti took the lead in formation of SHGs in Kalahandi District and KBK region. The findings of the study suggest that 50 per cent of sample SHGs were promoted by NGOs and financed by the banks under model-II. However, 19 per cent samples were promoted and linked directly by the banks under model-I and 25 per cent were promoted and financed indirectly under model-III. As many as 89,194 families in Kalahandi District got benefited in SHGs bank linkage programme. This helped to increase the income levels of families and has succeeded in migration, since the working of SHGs in 201-02.

A study by APMAS (2005) on SHG-Bank linkage in Andhra Pradesh Mahila Abhivrudhi Society (APMAS) suggests that more than 50 per cent of the SHGs bank linkage in the country are in Andhra Pradesh. The socio-economic status of women has increased after participating in the SHGs actitivies which helped the members to earn and contribute to the family income. It has also empowered women to take part themselves in other development programmes. The level of confidence, self-reliance, ability to make decisions and the leadership quality of women has increased due to the participation in the SHGs movement initiated in Andhra Pradesh.

Study by Mishra, R.K. (2007) on Micro-finance: Challenges Ahead suggests that there has been a great improvement in the social capital with the introduction of micro-finance into the lives of the poor. The trick in micro-finance lies not in taking giant leaps but in taking small steps to cover a long distance.

Relevance of the Study

The country has more than two decades experience in working with about five million SHGs promoted by different agencies. Though the objectives and approaches of promoting agencies are different, the ultimate goal is to improve the quality of life of the poor in the rural areas. In fact, it must be admitted that, thrift and credit activity continues to be the lifeline of SHG. The SHG formation provides for all encompassing environment, for conscious management, development, decentralize decision-making, transparency in transactions and encouragement of resource poor groups for sustainable group action, and enterprise development among the rural poor. Most of the studies are concerned with social aspects of the SHG formation, working, bank linkages and their impact on empowerment. The economic impact of SHG has not been much emphasized. There is no such study in Orissa for undertaking the development and implementation of SHGs on economic activities of women in state of Orissa.

The present study is taken up with an objective to examine the existing process of group formation under SHGs and its impact on the economic status of women in the State of Orissa. The study is designed to identify some key factors which can promote strong, self-relient, pro-active and sustainable groups for enhancing the livelihood security among the group members of SHGs in Orissa to assess the strength and weakness of SHG approach in Orissa.

Objectives and Scope of the Study

The primary objective of the study is to analyse the present status of SHGs and its impact on economic stuats of women in Orissa. Some of the specific objectives of current study are:

1. To ascertain the socio-economic profile of the SHGs and their members under micro-finance.
2. To examine the SHG bank-linkage programme for ensuring financial services for members and groups for undertaking economic activities to generate sustainable livelihood.
3. To study the impact of bank-linkage on women participation.
4. To assess the participation of SHG members in other related development programmes for ensuring empowerment of women in Orissa.

The spectrum of the analysis is confined to banks and NGOs in financing SHGs. The field of the study is limited for the State of Orissa. However, a sketchy reference of Andhra Pradesh is made with regard to Women Self-help Groups as they have been a marked success in the sphere of women empowerment. Due to resource and time constraint, the present study concentrates merely economic aspect of empowerment of women. In economic aspect, literacy, occupational status and health level of women are focused. The study covers in development of micro-finance and economic empowerment of women in Orissa for one decade.

Hypotheses of the Study

The study aims at testing a set of hypotheses with the help of finding evaluation. After analysis, the following hypotheses are to be tested either to conform or reject:

1. Formation of SHGs has a positive impact on enhancement economic status of women in the family and in the society.
2. The micro-finance of SHG in Orissa is an innovative endeavour to provide sustainable livelihood security to women.
3. The rural women members have the perception that they will develop and minimize exploitation to them on joining SHG movements in the villages.
4. The SHG is an alternative model for development and empowerment of women in Orissa.
5. The SHG movement might have a negative impact on the family relationship as the women members engaged in participation of group activities outside their village.

Methodology of the Study

Methodology applied for the study is illustrated below:

1. **Collection of data:** The present study is based on both primary and secondary data. The primary data were collected through a field survey with the help of a structural questionnaire. The primary data are to be used to assess the socio-economic conditions of SHGs and their members of the group and to examine the impact of SHG on the economic status of women in Orissa.

   The Secondary data were collected from the published secondary sources i.e. plan documents, published reports, standard texts, etc. The secondary data were used to analyse the growth of SHG movement in

Orissa and to examine the SHG bank-linkage programme for functioning of the group to ensure the sustainability of activities.

2. **Sampling design:** For the purpose of sampling, it has been decided to choose the SHGs and women empowerment in Orissa. The data will be taken on the basis of representative sampling instead of taking the whole universe. For the purpose of the study, five hundred (500) sample households are to be taken by using systematic random sampling method. The primary data were supplemented and cross-checked by secondary data assembled from Economic Survey, Government of Orissa, 2007-08, District Statistical Hand Book, statistical abstracts of Orissa, 2007, issues of EPW, conference volume of Indian Economic Association, Indian journal of Commerce, dailies like *Times of India* and interviews with official concerned.

REFERENCES

Dhar, P.K., "*Indian Economy and Its Growing Dimensions*, Kalyani Publishers, New Delhi, 2006".

Dutta, Rudra and Sundaram K.P.M, *Indian Economy*, Sultan Chand & Co., New Delhi, 2005.

Falendra, K. Sudan, "Empowering Rural Women Through Micro Enterprise Development", Social Change and Development Vol. 3, July 2005, pp. 54-73.

Ghule and V. Mahajan, "Micro-Finance – A Tool for Alleviation in the Globalised Scenario – Focus on Women SHGs", *Indian Commerce Bulletin*, December 2004, pp. 36-44.

Haque, Serajul, "Micro-Credit and Empowerment of Women: Evidence from Bangladesh", *Asian Economic Review*, December 2005, Vol. 47, No. 3, pp. 411-420.

Harper, Malcolm and Dr. Manoj Nath, "Inequity in the Self-Help Group Movement: A View from Ideas Centre", *Shelter*, January 2004, Vol. 7, No. 1, pp. 14-24.

Kole, Swapna and Arya Kumar, "Facilitating Entrepreneurship Amongst Rural Women: Issues and Challenges", *Asian Economic Review*, December 2005, Vol. 47, No. 3, pp. 445-455.

Kullur, M.S. and Biradar, A.A., "The New Paradigm of Micro-finance and the Role of Non-governmental Voluntary Agencies in its Promotion: A Few Reflections", *In NGOs and Socio-economic Development Opportunities* (ed) Kanta Prasad, Deep and Deep Publications, New Delhi, 2000.

Kumar, D. and Shanuga Sundaram A., "Role of Women Self-Help Groups in Rural Poverty Alleviation: With Special Reference to Nankal District of Tamil Nadu", In: K.K. Bagche (ed), *Employment and Poverty Alleviation Programmes in India*, Abhijeet Publications, 2007.

Manabsen, "Micro-Finance and Self-help Groups: An Alternative Social Economic Option for the Poor", In: Kanta Prasad (ed) *NGOs and Socio-Economic Development Opportunities*, Deep & Deep Publications, New Delhi.

Mishra, R.N., *Women Education and Development*, Discovery Publishing House, Pvt. Ltd., New Delhi, 2006.

Mohanty, B.B., Sudhdeve M.L. and Manikumar S., "Mega Socio-Economic Transformation thrill Micro-Finance The NABARD Experience", *Focus*, October 2005, pp. 9-22.

Reddy, Y.V., "Micro-Finance: Reserve Bank's Approach, *RBI Bulletin* September 2005, pp. 841-846.

Sarangi, Prasant., "Micro-Finance, Empowerment of Women Self-Help Groups", In: S.N. Tripathy (ed), *Women and Rural Development*, Discovery Publishing House Pvt. Ltd., New Delhi, 2005.

Seilan, A., "Micro-Finance Through SHG: An Innovative Method of Banking with the Unbankables", *Hindecon* 2004, pp. 122-126.

Yunus, Muhammad, "Grameen Bank, Micro-Credit and Millennium Development Goals", *Economic and Political Weekly*, September 4, 2004, pp. 4077-4080.

2

Micro-finance and Self-help Groups

Dr. Sudhakar Patra*

For a country as diverse as India with its vast size, heterogeneous culture, large-scale inequality any centralized planning targeting a group for alleviating their poverty is bound to be a failure. If we scan the different anti-poverty programmes we will find in all the cases the failure is attributed to the non-participation or non-inclusiveness of target groups. The problem was compounded after India became a globalized economy. Globalization resulted in high economic growth rate with higher level of concentration of economic power with fewer hands. In this context it would be pertinent to follow the path of Prof. Muhammad Yunus who received Nobel Prize for peace for his contribution to economics . Prof Yunus has subtly related economics with peace by stating , "peace prevails only when hunger is quelled." Prof Yunus started Grameen Bank in 1974 in Bangladesh only with a view to deal with micro-credit which he believed will ultimately reach to the target groups. India with around 60,000 Bank branches, with fourth largest banking infrastructure in the world but 94 per cent of the six lakh villages do not have a single branch. So if small farmers, artisans, traders of small means

* **Reader in Economics, Ravenshaw University, Cuttack, (Orissa).**

and rag pickers have been able to improve their lives in any manner today, it is because of Self-help Groups (SHGs) and Micro-finance institutions. The Paradigm Shift in extending micro-credit Which leads to inclusive growth was spawned by micro-finance. The SHG-Bank linkage took shape in 1986 by National Bank for Agriculture and Rural Development (NABARD) when it lend its first formal loan to MYRADA, a voluntary organisation in Karnataka, which in turn helped in the formation of large SHGs. Poverty is the most excruciating blasphemy of human dignity. The majority of the poor is living in rural India and the women are its main component. Poverty has taken the shape of 'Feminization of Poverty' in the country. With this awareness, the Planning Commission has focused on women empowerment. To wage a direct war against poverty, the Government has introduced Self-help Group Programme as an innovative and dynamic anti-poverty programme. The NABARD is the main initiator of SHGs. Of late, both Central and State Governments, nationalized commercial banks, regional rural banks, Co-operative banks and societies and NGOs have joined the SHG movement as promoters. The SHG are the best facilitators of rural employment and income generation, income distribution and empowerment of rural women. The basic objective of the SHGs formed by women is to "help constrict a society which is: self-reliant, conscious of social-economic issues, where there is a spirit of co-operative, where women are appropriately skilled to undertake their choice of activities without hindrances or dependence, where there is a leadership development which maintaining gender equality and above all each having a respect for the values of others and each striving for good of the greater society."

The emergence and rapid multiplication of SHGs based on micro-credit is a phenomenon that is gaining increasing importance in the development scenario. The SHGs have been viewed by the State as a strategy both women's empowerment as well as poverty reduction. The NGOs have increasingly been adopting SHGs as a strategy to bring women together, at a faster pace and larger scale than the collective building processes adopted by then earlier. But it is also a hard truth that slowly and slowly the groups have become only the means of collection and distribution of savings among the members and other activities related to women development have become secondary. There are many factors responsible for lowering the effectiveness of these groups via, illiteracy, lake of proper leadership, management, promotion of income generating activities etc.

Credit Needs and Emerging Challenges

Credit is a right that poor women must have access to. The experience and studies of SHGs reveals that although they have provided improved access to credit it is not affordable credit. Poor women pool in their resources and access credit for crisis and consumption (mostly food, health and education). Although participation in SHGs has meant opportunities related to mobility and a legitimate space in the public realm for leaders of SHGs, the overall picture is one that raises several critical concerns related to gender justice, livelihoods and empowerment which needs to be addressed.

It cannot be limited to merely forming of SHGs and providing access to credit. It cannot substitute the role of development and growth in other sectors and cannot be an excuse for reducing state expenditure on social sector. By projecting the SHGs involved in savings and credit activities as the most effective way to deal with poverty. The benefits of SHGs for improvement in livelihoods situation can be analysed from following points:

1. The SHG members have little control over financial resources that they borrow despite being the conduit for access to such credit through their groups. These have at best yielded supplementary incomes, insufficient to bring families out of poverty.

2. The micro-enterprise activities undertaken have tended to be unviable in the absence of inputs related to infrastructure, marketing and capacity building. Low levels of credit absorption capacity, low skill base and low asset base have been challenges to the SHG movement, which are yet to be addressed.

3. There continue to be serious hurdles faced by women when they want to access credit from banks, despite claims to the contrary.

4. The total quantum of credit available to men however continues to be larger both in outreach and quantum/ or in aggregate and per capita as farmers and entrepreneurs.

5. Women being pressurized by banks to recover loans made earlier to men in the village as an unwritten conditionality before loans are released to them.

6. The fundamental livelihoods concerns related to the existing economic realities (such as those related to agriculture or natural resources) of poor women's lives remain largely unaddressed in the process.

7. Access to credit as the focus of the micro-credit programmes looses sight of the issues fundamental issues of access and control over common resources such as water forests, etc. which are the mainstay of occupations of a large number of the rural poor.

8. Lack of skills/experience for advisory/technical support services to promote livelihoods and build sustainable interventions among the intermediary organizations especially NGOs etc.

Exclusion of the Poorest and Defunct Groups

The norms of the amount to be saved and regularity of saving are often set by sponsors of the SHGs with a view to making the SHG self-sustainable which has led to the exclusion of the poorest, including members from Dalit, tribal and Muslim communities, migrant workers as well as women headed households from the SHGs most interior and tribal villages have not benefited. On the other hand women's organisations that have been actively engaged in mobilisation on survival issues prior to the onset of the popular SHG formations are not recognised as effective forums. The rapid growth of SHGs combined with inadequate support being provided to them has meant that a large number of groups are defunct and exist only on paper. The pressure of targets has meant that there are multiple claims being made on SHG members by different sponsoring agencies, thereby exaggerating the number of women being covered by SHGs.

Lack of support to address inequity and gender injustice:

1. The agenda of SHGs most often fails to include social justice and equity issues, although women may take up issues related to violence against women even in the absence of support from the sponsoring agency.
2. Members of SHGs are also making demands from governance institutions often without success.
3. Although it is recognised that literacy is an important factor, capacity-building inputs to develop literacy skills are very limited.
4. Women experience invisible barriers to entry in economic and political spheres.

Accountability and Capacity Building

The SHGs find that when they need support they find that existing governance systems are not accountable to them. Most often the government programmes tend to subvert the Panchayati Raj Institutions (PRI) from where the SHGs could potentially seek redressal of their grievances. While SHGs serve the interests of numerous institutional players such as the State (including in the delivery of development messages and schemes), banks and corporations, there is grossly insufficient ploughing back of any resources for the women themselves, either for crisis support or for their capacity building. This is despite the fact that information, skills, attitudinal change and perspective building are corner stones of empowerment and poverty alleviation:

1. There are a large number of government sponsored SHGs that have not received any capacity building inputs. According to the survey of 2700 SHGs conducted by Nirantar 47 per cent of such groups formed by the government had not received inputs.
2. The capacity building inputs being provided are overwhelmingly focused on the cadre of sponsoring agencies and fail to reach SHG members.
3. Inputs on social justice and equity issues, either do not reach SHGs or if they do it is in a highly diluted manner. The overwhelming focus is on the functional agenda related to group formation and ensuring regular savings and repayment.
4. Amongst SHG members it is group leaders (who are the more educated) who are receiving inputs.
5. When issues related to gender are included in the group leader trainings, they receive only tokenistic attention.

Micro-credit is only one of the inputs and enabling conditions that is required for empowerment and poverty alleviation. The State in particular needs to invest adequate resources and to change policies in a manner that women's subordinate status and poverty is addressed. It has been seen that any programme of whatever magnitude and kind starts diminishing once the agencies and schemes start with drawing. It order to constantly boost up the spirits of members and build trust of confidence among them, some functional recommendations are given here under:

1. Promotion of literacy among members.
2. Proper organization and management of group.
3. Leadership development.
4. Exposure-cum-learning visits.
5. Information empowerment.
6. Technological interventions.
7. Activate groups in Social mobilization.
8. Promotion of Income generating Activities.
9. Evaluation, Impact Study and Follow up.
10. Organizational linkage development.

Self-help Groups

Nothing will better help anybody than his own self-government has devised many programmes to uplift the poor particularly in the economic front. One such measure is the formation of self-help groups and NABARD under the guidance of Reserve Bank of India has devised strategies for providing financial support to the SHGs for the economic growth in general and economic emancipation of rural poor women folk in particular. Though SHGs are not meant only for women, men can also form SHGs but no doubt more emphasis has been laid in the women.

The self-help groups are voluntary associations or groups small in size, autonomous and most importantly non-political. It is formed by, small and marginal farmers, artisans and traders of small means and land less labourers. Forming a homogeneous back ground with respect to origin, heritage, culture SHGs operate on the principle of co-operation and mutual trust. Each SHGs is formed by 10-20 poor persons belonging to a particular locality. They elect among them their office bearers. They are completely independent and no body except the members would have a say on the maintenance of SHGs. There is complete cohesion among the members and transparency in the accounts as the account is small. The members collect small savings from among them and lend the same to its members and the residual amount is deposited in the banks. The bank SHG Co-operation is doing exceedingly well in Orissa. The block machinery help in the formation of SHGs by educating them about the advantages of formation of such groups. The big thing about it is that it needs no registration of any SHG under any society act.

In Orissa Misson Shakti has been launched on march 2001 by the Chief Minister to give micro-finance to one lakh SHGs by March 2005 and two lakh SHGs for empowerment of women in Orissa. NABARD and MISSION SHAKTI directorate are working in tandem to ensure economic growth and create a paradigm shift in economic development via economic emancipation of poor women.

Objectives of Self-help Groups

There are multiple objectives of SHGs out of which important objectives are as follows:

1. To help construct a society which is self-reliant.
2. To ensure consciousness of socio-economic issues.
3. To create the spirit of co-operation.
4. To facilitate finance to take up any micro project for income generation without any hindrance.
5. To build mutual trust between the banker and the rural poor.
6. To encourage small saving which otherwise would not have been tapped.
7. To evolve strategies for providing micro-finance to its members.
8. To encourage banking habit among rural poor.

Activities of SHGs

The important activities of SHGs are stated below:

1. Collection of savings.
2. Disbursement of credits.
3. Earns interest through its normal business.
4. Depositing savings in the NGO/Bank.
5. Creates linkage between bank & SHG members.
6. Helps sanction to loans to its members from bank.
7. Exerts pressure on recoveries.
8. Arranges marketing of products.
9. Arranges training of its members.
10. Helps producing kitchen products like pickles etc.

SHGs in Micro-credit Delivery System

The failures of the past developmental efforts are largely attributed to the lack of people's participation. In response to it, the emphasis shifted to local development with the people's participation. It has come to be recognised as an absolute imperative for development. Some even argue that development, in fact is participation (Prasad, 2002). It has been recognised that economic development of women is possible through their active participation in the development process. In this regard, SHGs are considered as a viable alternative to achieve the development and to get the community participation in all round development programmes. From humble beginning micro-finance has come to occupy a pivotal position in rural credit. The Indian micro-finance scene is dominated by SHGs and their linkage to banks. Credit delivery through thrift and credit groups (SHGs) emerge an alternative to the existing system of credit disbursement by the banks, unlike most government credit programmes, deposit mobilisation is prominent in thrift based self-help groups.

SHG-Bank Linkage and Role of NGOs

The NABARD launched its SHG-Bank linkage programme in 1991-92. It is operational in nearly 20 States in India and is actively channellising credit to the poorer sections of the society for mainly non-farm activities. During its inception it started with 255 SHGs and it has reached to 94,645 groups by March 2000. Approximately 8.25 million families are benefited by the linkage programme by 1998. In all the 85 per cent of the groups linked with banks are formed exclusively by women (NABARD 2000).

A total of 26 Commercial Banks and 46 Regional Rural Banks have been participated in the linkage programme. The experiments of the linkage programme were conducted through different models as mentioned below:

(a) **Model I:** Banks lend directly to the ultimate borrowers without having NGOs/Self-help Promoting Institutions (SHPIs) and SHGs as intermediary.

(b) **Model II:** Banks lend directly to the borrowers by forming SHGs.

(c) **Model III:** Banks lend to SHGs to lend to borrowers with NGOs/SHPIs as non-financial intermediaries.

(d) **Model IV:** Banks give credit to NGOs/SHPIs to lend to SHGs to lend to the ultimate borrowers.

The past experience shows that rural populations particularly those who belong to poor and weaker sections and women, could not avail the benefits of development due to illiteracy, poverty, social conflicts etc. In order to create awareness, educate and motivate among these people the NGOs, play a very crucial role. In order to assess the role of NGOs in the micro credit delivery system as well as for the overall economic empowerment of women the researcher has taken PREM (a local NGO) for the study purpose.

REFERENCES

Agarwal, Bina. "*Economic Participation of Rural Women in the Third World*", *EPW*, A-155-A-163.

Bhatia, Anju. (2000). "*Womens Development and NGOs*", Rawat Publications, New Delhi.

Das, Vidya (1991). "*Bilateral Funding and Women's Empowerment*", *EPW*, Vol. XXVI, Nos. 22 & 23, June.

Das, A.K. (1995), "*NGOs and Development: Learning from Failures*", *The Fourth World*, No. 2, p. 74.

George, J. (1993). "*Adjustment with Gender Equallity", Mainstream*, Vol. XXXI, No. 20, March 27.

Ghosh, D.K. (2001). "*NGO Intervention in Poverty Alleviation: Scope and Reality*", *Kurukshetra*, Vol. 49, No. 6, pp. 2-10.

Government of India, (2000). *Women in India: A Statistical Profile, Women in Partnership with Men*, Planning Commission, New Delhi.

Government of Orissa (1999). Report, *State Commission for Women*, Bhubaneswar.

NABARD, Various Reports: 1997, 1998, 1999 and 2000.

Various Reports of PREM.

Prasad, K, (2002) "*NGOs and Social Development Opportunities*" (ed.) Volume.

The Hindu (1999).

3

Self-help Groups and Economic Empowerment of Tribal Women

Dr. Kabita Kumari Sahu*

Abstract

The chapter seeks to analyze the achievements, prospects and challenges of Micro-finance and self-help groups of tribal women in a tribal dominated Mayurbhanj district of Orissa with the help of secondary and primary data on number of tribal women, self-help groups, members, savings, bank accounts opened with credit linkages, grading and income generating activities created in 26 blocks. The facilitating role played by Banks, NGOs, Mission Shakti, ICDS, Block officers are focused with revolving fund, federations and credit unions for on lending to tribal women SHGs for promoting micro-finance. The chapter also discusses on capacity building, group entrepreneurship development of tribal women through income generating activities of SHG members like candle & pickle making, retail and wholesale trading, fishing etc. A comparative

* **Lecturer in Economics, North Orissa University, Baripada (Orissa).**

analysis of growth and performance of tribal women SHGs is also provided with reference to saving, credit, repayment position, default, credit diversion and bank linkages along with deposit and lending interest rates. A tribal agency model linking post offices to SHGs for micro-finance is also analysed with many suggestions for improving micro-finance in Orissa for economic empowerment of rural poor tribal women.

Introduction

Tribal women live in distant villages located amidst hilly forested regions and their life is integrally linked to the forest for their food, fodder and wood for fuel. These tribal women have always remained invisible, forgotten, marginalized, deprived and unrecognized. The development ideology pursued in India after independence has ruthlessly damaged and destroyed vast tracts of forest leading to the erosion of a life support system, displacement from their ancestral lands and loss of control of and access to a wide variety of forest resources. The disappearance of people based practices like agro-forestry and food gathering has specifically and adversely affected the lives of tribal women which increased their daily drudgery by manifold times. The displacement due to larger development projects, non-access, non-possession, non-entitlement have further forced these tribal women into mute acceptance.

Micro-finance is emerging as a powerful instrument for empowerment of poor, particularly tribal women both socially and economically. It aims at providing cost effecting mechanism for financial services to the unreached tribal poor women. Empowerment is a process of change by which individuals or groups gain power and ability to take control over their lives. It involves increased well-being, access to resources, rising self confidence, increasing participation in decision-making and control over resources and lives. The women empowerment has received extensive recognition as a strategy of growth and poverty reduction. Before 1990 credit schemes for rural tribal women were almost negligible. The concept of women's credit was recognised by women-oriented studies who recommended access to credit by the poor tribal women in informal sector. In modern economy the micro credit approach for women is considered as the best strategy to empower women economically. Through micro-credit the poor women can rotate their funds to build economic capacities and capabilities. The world women conference at Helsinky has rightly recognised the credit scheme for rural women as the best technique of women empowerment. The co-relation between credit and empowerment is always positive which has been established in all research studies. Whether income creation has any impact on women's poverty or payback women in development, the case is argued that micro-credit does not fulfil its claims of financially viable empowerment (Poster and Salima, 2002). But this perspective is criticized for taking too constricted view of poverty which is concerned with lack of money but others take a more encircling view (Sen, 1999). If help groups as local activity and group entrepreneurship may donate to women empowerment and nationality outcomes for poor tribal women at the local level (Robertson, 1995). Micro-finance through self-help groups may promote women's capacity to achieve and to create choices. It has been widely accepted that micro-finance programme and SHG would be very effective in poverty eradication and tribal women empowerment, if implemented in the right sense. In this context this article analyses the performance of women Self-Help Groups consisting of poor tribal women in Mayurbhanj district of Orissa where about 57 per cent of population are scheduled tribes.

Mission Shakti and Empowerment of Tribal Women

Mission Shakti Scheme was launched in Mayurbhanj district on 3rd May, 2001. The mission aims at empowering women through formation and promotion of women's Self-help Groups. The banks also provide institutional credit to the SHGs to take up various income generating activities. The NABARD is playing a promotional role in this regard. Organization of women as SHGs in tribal areas have also brought a silent revolution in the rural areas. These groups are taking up social issues like dowry prohibition, illicit liquor trade etc. Over 25 lakhs people have organized themselves under 2.05 lakhs self-help groups. Significantly, out of these about 19.88 lakh are women, who have formed as many as 1.58 lakh all-women groups to achieve women empowerment, has now become a buzzword in rural Orissa, as members venture into income generation and social reforms, education and health awareness. With bank credit flowing into the sector, women SHGs have expanded their economic activities. They run cooking gas agencies of IOC and BPCL, besides kerosene dealerships of the State public distribution system. The multi-national consumer goods manufacturer, Hindustan Levers Ltd (HLL) has been distributing its products in the rural areas though 1000 women SHGs as its dealers. With their purses bulging, women members now buy insurance covers for themselves as social security. Over 44,408 SHGs have taken Janashree Bima Policy of the Life Insurance Corp (LIC). Only Rs. 175.39 crore has reached 1.47 lakh women SHGs entitled to bank credit in 2004-05, as against their own savings of Rs 110.81 crore. Public sector banks, regional rural banks (RRBs) and cooperative banks provide micro credit, while private banks are yet to begin.

With a marketing network in place in coming years, Mission Shakti will be the biggest movement in the State to eradicate poverty and for the empowerment of women. The SHGs are likely to make village moneylenders jobless, and would be able to do away with the middle man in trade, if bank credit is adequate and the marketing network functions efficiently. The Government of Orissa decided to implement the targeted rural initiative for poverty termination and infrastructure (TRIPTI), a World Bank-aided programme under Orissa Poverty Reduction Mission, through Mission Shakti which is working for the economic uplift of rural poor women. India is notable for the self-help group (SHG) bank linkage movement which has helped to bring financial services to large numbers of poor people. The SHGs are member-owned and controlled financial service enterprises, providing savings and credit services to their members. They usually distribute their profits to members and they facilitate members' access to education and training. They are, in effect, micro-cooperatives. They are linked to bigger financial institutions to keep their savings and provide additional capital for on-lending to members. The SHGs have increasingly been seen as good business for banks - they are a source of deposits and reliable at repaying loans.

Micro-finance and Women Empowerment

Given the widespread gender bias against women in different fields, there are arguments that interventions like micro-finance have the potential to enhance women's capabilities which can make significant difference to overall development of women. Those who hold the above view argue for supporting micro-finance interventions and tuning them to meet the needs of women specifically. On the other hand, there are arguments that micro-finance interventions can at best have only a very limited impact in empowering women. Interventions such as micro-finance are constrained by the existing socio-cultural structures such as patriarchy in order for them to make a very significant impact on women. Under such circumstances women hardly have any control in deciding or directing loan use for purposes, which can enhance their individual economic position over those dictated by familiar requirements. Access to savings and credit can take care of mainly the practical needs of women instead of meeting their strategic needs. A study which looked at the changes brought about by longer association of members with their SHGs concluded that members of the old SHGs emerged as more confident, financially more secure, more in control of their lives, and in a stronger position *vis-à-vis* their family members. The personal abilities, ownership of economic assets, development of skills, ability to decide about self and extent of participation in political sphere are likely to participate in SHGs for a longer period. At the same time, there evidence which tell us that micro-finance and SHGs may not always lead to transformational impact on women. A study found that women have certainly become more visible as micro-finance clients, but being a client doesn't translate automatically into empowerment. The study found only mixed evidence about the role of micro-finance in either increasing women's economic activity or increasing women's awareness, mobility and skill development or enhance women's and decision-makers. The study however, observed that between different models of micro-finance, the SHG model seems to show better scope for developing women's opportunities and skills. Micro-finance is emerging as a powerful instrument for poverty alleviation in the new economy. In India, micro-finance scene is dominated by SHGs-Bank linkage programme, aimed at providing a cost effective mechanism for providing financial services to the unreached poor. Based on the philosophy of group saving as collateral substitute, the SHG Programme has been successful in not only in meeting peculiar needs of the rural poor, but also in strengthening collective self-help capacities of the poor at the local level, leading to the empowerment.

Empowerment is a process of change by which individuals or groups gain power and ability to take control over their lives. It involves increased well-being, access to resources, increased self-confidence, self-esteem and respect, increased participation in decision-making and bargaining power and increased control over benefits, resources and own life. Micro-finance programmes tend to focus on promoting changes at the individual level. However, the scope for empowerment of individual women is usually limited by inequalities and discrimination women face collectively. Women's empowerment thus requires addressing women's status and women's rights as a group in order to enable women to make use of resources.

Micro-credit for the poor and women has received extensive recognition as a strategy for poverty reduction and for economic empowerment. Increasingly in the past five years, there is a questioning of whether micro-credit is the most effective approach to economic empowerment of the poorest and among them, women in particular. Development practitioners in India and developing countries often argue that the exaggerated focus on micro-credit as a solution for the poor has owed to neglect by the State and public institutions in addressing employment and livelihood needs of the poor. With the onset of structural adjustment programmes in the early nineties, there was a public debate around reduced state spending on social sectors. In a country like India, economic uncertainties, loss of livelihood, inflation, lack of access to natural resources, declining employment, increasing social unrest, natural disaster, etc. make the poor extremely vulnerable. In this context it would be necessary to ensure that the poor are empowered to access development resources and use it to their greatest benefit.

Micro-finance and Tribal Women Self-help Groups in Mayurbhanj

Mayurbhanj is a land locked district covering an area of 10,41,800 sq. km which is the largest among all the 30 districts of State and bounded by Balasore district in the east, Keonjhar and Balasore districts in the south, Midnapore district of West Bengal and Singbhum district of Jharkhand in the north and by Singbhum and Keonjhar in the north. According to 2001 census, the total population of Mayurbhanj district is 22,23,456 and it consists of 4 Subdivisions, 9 Tahasils, 382 Gram Panchayats, 26 Community Development Blocks, 28 police stations, 1 Municipality, 3 NACs and 3950 villages among which 3748 villages are inhabited and 202 villages are uninhabited, 6 Fire stations, 4 towns, 26 C.D blocks and 10 Assembly Constituencies. The district is at a height of 559.31 metres above the sea level. The main river of the district is the Budhabalanga and the area of the district is 4243 sq. miles which is rich in varieties of soil and sights. Mayurbhanj covers a huge part of forest area of the State. In this district the reserve forest is 3330.14 sq. km. The district occupies the Third position in the State after Kandhamal and Sundargarh so far as percentage of forest the State is concerned. Moreover, the Similipal forest of Mayurbhanj district comprising a single compact block represented a virgin and semi evergreen forest with flora and fauna.

Due to poverty the rural people, particularly tribal women of Mayurbhanj have taken keen interest in formation of self-help groups. The Mission Shakti is actively engaged along with many non-governmental organizations in formation of self-help groups for women. There are 26 administrative blocks in the district and the total number of WSHGS in the district are 18,016. The highest number of WSHGS are found in Kaptipada Block (807) followed by 1032 WSHGS in Badasahi block.

In Baripada District Headquarters there are only 816 WSHGS and lowest WSHGs is 335 in Tiring Block. The detail physical status of WSHGs in different blocks are presented in Table 3.1. The ICDS is the main agency in the District who is playing the leading role in formation of Self-Help Groups. It has formed more than 60% of total SHGs and the members are highest in Moroda Block followed by

Betnoti Block. The Government officers and block administrative machinery are also playing vital role in formation of SHGs. The non-governmental organisations are forming 30 per cent of total WSHGs in the district. The Anganwadi workers are acting as the Secretary in most of the WSHGS and they are keeping records and playing the most important role in growth and performance of these groups.

Tribal Women Self-Help Groups and NGOs

There are many NGOs operating in Mayurbhanj district due to higher percentage of tribal and low literacy. Since 1991 these NGOs are actively involved in formation of WSHGs but their activities has increased after 2001 due to encouragement of Mission Shakti. Pradan a leading NGO has formed 242 WSHGs in Karanjia Block and Starr has formed 172 groups in Udala block. Unnayan has formed 81 groups in Rasgovindpur block. The detail list of NGOs and no. of groups formed are given in Table 3.2.

Financial Status of Women Self-help Groups

The basic objective of formation of these groups is to collect saving from the members and get credit linkage from the banks to provide micro-credit. In Mayurbhanj the cumulative amount of savings is not encouraging but the credit to the members is quite significant. The highest amount of saving from Women Self-Help Group is 180.38 thousand which is collected in Betnoti block followed by Badasahi and Suliapada blocks. Similarly the credit and bank linkage is quite significant in Udala, Bangriposi, Suliapada and Karanjia block. The detail amount of saving and credit is given in Table 3.3. It is a matter of fact that the number of women self-help groups is quite good in different blocks but the contribution of members for the group as saving is quite marginal. The commercial bank providing credit linkage should work hard in promoting these self-help groups.

Table 3.1: Physical Status of WSHGS in Mayurbhanj

Name of the Block	Total Comulative No. of WSHGs	ICDS		Block	
		No. of SHG Formed	No. of Members	No. of SHG Formed	No. of Members
1	2	3	4	5	6
Jashipur	623	402	4468	134	1640
Shamakhunta	805	715	8042	–	–
Morada	988	914	12923	25	290
Khunta	709	537	8413	14	155
Bijatala	357	354	3605	–	–
Jamda	388	383	4808	5	70
Thakurmunda	774	425	5409	9	117
Tiring	335	335	4459	–	–
Baripada	816	725	7417	13	150
Bishoi	546	474	5453	14	165
Udala	820	591	8803	12	162

(Contd...)

1	2	3	4	5	6
Bangiriposhi	832	690	750	—	—
Kuliana	810	645	7247	38	420
Kusumi	550	501	5120	12	120
Karanjia	838	546	5737	2	24
Suliapada	959	869	9360	19	120
Badasahi	1032	889	10218	44	24
Rasgovindpur	711	545	6945	23	200
Betnoti	1040	931	11224	58	502
Saraskana	770	684	6933	—	299
Bahalda	433	338	3494	54	823
Rairangpur	385	375	3945	5	—
Rarauan	515	372	4047	7	638
Sukruli	443	271	3075	55	60
Gopabandhunagar	640	569	7173	7	79
Kaptipada	807	764	8333	45	660

Table 3.2: WSHGs Formed by NGO

Name of the Block	Name of NGO (No. of WSHGs)
1	2
Jashipur	Spar (27), Creftda (10), Sambandh (33) Shankari (8)
Shamakhunta	World Vision (30)
Morada	Piolet Project (3), M.M. Unnayan Samiti (8), MSJV, Sankhabhanga (5), TADA, Chitrada (5), WSSS Panchavaya (12)
Khunta	Gram Vikas (40), Badam Vikas (10), Sagen (27), Amarjyoti (28), Samaj Vikas (53), Rose (2) Loka Jagruti (2) Keso (1)
Bijatala	Pallivikas (3)
Thakurmunda	Sambandha (71), Lokashakti (20), Deep (25) Yojana (54), NYK (10), CYSD (42), BISWA (52) Kash (35) Orissa (10) Pradan (14)
Baripada	GVT (26), PMS (23), Sheba (1), Shakti (1), Gram Vikas (5), Khrisi Jyoti (3), VARD (2), Pilot Project (3)
Bishoi	Palli Chetana (12), Nari Rashmi Samaj (15), Udaya Bhanu Club (2), Dulala (9), Spar (6) Aid Orissa (5)
Udala	Starr (172), Arambha (15), Prava (9), Soova (6) JVO (14)
	(Contd...)

1	2
Bangiriposhi	Lamp (38), Olamp (12), Dulal (37), Palli Chetana (15), Gramin Vikas (12), AID (24), Maa Ambika S Vikas Society (4)
Kuliana	Dulal (48), Pallivikas (6), Maa Ambika Samaj Vikas Society (2), NYK (16), Sankalpa (12), Gram Nirman (4), G.V.T. (10), BNK (5), KHG (9), Janaseba Pratisthana (8)
Kusumi	Palli Shree (4) Gram Vikas (9), RDAC (7), Dulal (9)
Karanjia	Pradan (242), Lepra India (9), Biswa (15)
Sulipada	NYK (60) Samaj Seba (3)
Bada Sahi	Ford (14), CIDR (16)
Rasgovindpur	Unnayan (81) ACM (10) SKP (35) C.P. (17)
Betnoti	NYK Sangathana (5) Ford (10) Swadhina (10) PIDA (20) Dhan Foundation (6)
Saraskana	T & WD Society (12), AID (24) , Maa Ambika S Vikas Society (44)
Bahalda	Palli Chetana (12) Agragati Orissa (29)
Rairangpur	Gram Vikas (5)
Raruan	Agragati (39) Gram Vikas (62) Biswa (64)
Sukruli	Agragati (52), Biswa (1) Kash (30)
Gopabandhunagar	IM & T Society (15), Samaj Vikas (8)
Kaptipada	Dulal (13) Agrani (5) NSBSS (40) Anwesan (11), ACM (4)

* In Jamda and Tiring Bolcks, WSHGs are not formed by NGOs.

Table 3.3: Financial Status of WSHGs in Mayurbhanj

Name of the Block	Cumulative Savings (In Rs. Lakh)	No. of WSHGS	Credit Advanced (In Rs. Lakh)
Jashipur	52.97	333	144.4
Shamakhunta	67.46	516	147.51
Morada	54.69	672	211.25
Khunta	43.08	521	133.22
Bijatala	17.81	273	56.01
Jamda	39.95	297	72.7
Thakurmunda	57.22	496	77.68
Tiring	16.06	299	76.35
Baripada	63.74	750	256.55
Bishoi	31.61	414	96.92
Udala	66.75	758	304.06
Bangiriposhi	57.50	642	314.46
Kuliana	100.31	555	388.82
Kusumi	35.57	385	197.31
Karanjia	42.27	699	351.87
Suliapada	97.89	798	445.55
Badasahi	115.68	915	374.1
Rasgovindpir	42.98	467	176.19
Betnoti	180.38	990	382.47
Saraskana	40.23	527	197.31
Bahalda	48.17	329	126.66
Rairangpur	43.10	290	142.61
Rarauan	30.75	417	89.02
Sukruli	15.18	385	98.95
Gopabandhunagar	44.03	382	70.02
Kaptipada	66.81	606	153.60
Total	**1514.19**	**13716**	**5055.59**

Gradation of Tribal Women Self-help Groups

Gradation reflects the performance assessment of groups in India. Out of 18,016 WSHGS, 7242 groups are in A grade, 5707 in B grade, 2230 in C grade and 1517 are in D grade. A total of 2837 groups are yet to be graded in Mayurbhanj district. In Betnoti block highest number of WSHGs (615) is in A grade which shows better performance in this block. Jamda block has the lowest performance with only 63 groups in A grade. In Jashipur block a highest number of WSHGs are yet to be graded. Under SGSY the highest finance is provided in Badasahi block followed by Kaptipada and Betanoti block. The detail gradation and finance under SGSY are given in Table 3.4.

Conclusion

The SHGs are playing a vital role in the development of rural credit system and empowerment of tribal rural women. The NABARD released a pilot project in 1992 encouraging the Banks to finance SHGs. Mission Shakti has been launched on 8th March, 2001 to give micro-finance to one lakh SHGs by March 2005 for empowerment of women in Orissa. The SHGs are facing a lot of difficulties in their time of working. The interference of male and local leaders really harsh the tribal women working in the WSHGs. Inadequate leadership, lack of operation of rules, inadequate bank credit linkage are the main causes of unsatisfactory performance of tribal WSHGs in Mayurbhanj. There are many functional problems like inefficient record keeping, corruption and mismanagement, lack of training, timely non-repayment of loans and lack of adequate marketing facilities which create difficulties for tribal WSHGs. The study reveals that tribal women SHGs are performing better in Mayurbhanj District in comparison to non-tribal WSHGs and they builds mutual trust and confidence between bankers and the rural poor. The share capital collected from the members of SHGs is extremely low

Table 3.4: Gradation of WSHGs in Mayurbhanj

Name of the Block	Total No. of SHGs	Gradation				Balance No. of SHGs to be Graded	SHGs Financed Under SGHY (Cumulative)	
		A	B	C	D		No. of SHGs	Amount
1	2	3	4	5	6	7	8	9
Jashipur	623	134	125	148	407	216	95	86.07
Shamakhunta	805	369	230	121	720	85	141	164
Morada	988	214	410	182	806	182	437	280.62
Khunta	709	258	344	50	655	54	238	156.76
Bijatala	357	248	67	8	323	34	116	92.22
Jamda	388	63	104	176	343	45	136	47.85
Thakurmunda	774	392	158	40	590	184	90	106.56
Tiring	335	273	20	6	299	36	142	178.65
Baripada	816	288	264	47	590	217	158	146.20
Bishoi	546	170	311	50	531	15	120	126.02

(Contd...)

1	2	3	4	5	6	7	8	9
Udala	820	242	321	99	662	158	313	11.02
Bangiriposhi	832	245	277	120	642	190	301	218.84
Kuliana	810	513	172	103	788	22	205	370.51
Kusumi	550	178	146	63	387	163	181	142.18
Karanjia	838	341	226	65	632	206	123	150.90
Suliapada	959	453	321	171	945	14	204	207.55
Badasahi	1032	408	388	216	1012	20	815	363.05
Rasgovindpur	711	255	159	5	419	292	241	146.40
Betnoti	1040	615	198	32	845	195	320	273.78
Saraskana	770	158	418	65	641	129	169	175.04
Bahalda	433	160	140	112	412	21	94	88.77
Rairangpur	385	203	133	38	374	11	185	150.33
Rarauan	515	362	118	31	511	4	202	125.17
Sukruli	443	241	135	12	388	55	144	65.31
Gopabandunagar	640	252	150	80	482	158	137	118.29
Kaptipada	897	207	369	190	766	131	231	274.68
Total	**18016**	**7242**	**5707**	**2230**	**5177**	**2837**	**5538**	**4366.77**

in Mayurbhanj. The women SHGs are performing better in Baripada and Betanati block. The members of SHGs avail loan regularly from the bank but not repay the loan due to poor economic condition. The post offices should be linked to tribal WSHGs for micro credit and deposits. The role of NGO in promoting tribal WSHGs in different stages is quite satisfactory. By linking with banks they encourage banking activities and evolve supplementary credit strategies for meeting the credit needs of the tribal women. The WSHGs are the rays of hopes which have become a prevailing, imperative and valuable means for face lifting, rejuvenating and empowering poor tribal women.

REFERENCES

Das, R.M.(2004), "Micro-Finance Through SHGs. A Boon for the Rural Poor". *Kurukshetra* Vol. 52, No. 4 February.

Das, S (2003): Self-Help Hroups Micro Credit: Synergic Integration, *Kurukshetra*, August, Vol. 51, No. 10.

Das, S.K., Nanda B.P and Rath J (2008): *Micro-finance and Rural Development in India*, Edited Book, New Century Publication, New Delhi.

Gangaiah C. Nagaraj B and Naidu C.V (2006): Impact of Self-Help Groups on Income and Employment, A Case Study, *Kurukshetra*, March, Vol. 54, No. 5.

Government of Orissa (2008): *Economic Survey of Orissa*, Ch. 9.

Government of Orissa (2006): *District Statistical Handbook*, Mayurbhanj.

Lalrinliana, J., and Kanayaraj F. (2006): SHGs and Tribal Development in Mizoram, *Kurukhetra*, January, Vol. 54, No. 3.

Loganathan, P. & Ashokan R. (2006): Inter Regional Development of Self-Help Groups in India, *Kurukshetra*, September, Vol. 54, No. 11.

Patra, S. (1998): Issues and Problems of Co-operatives, *Orissa Economic Journal*, Vol. XXXI.

Poster, W. and Salima Z (2002): The Limits of Micro Credit: Transnational Feminism and USAID Activities in the United

States and Morocco. In: N. Naples and M. Desai eds., Women's Activitism and Globalization: Linking Local Struggles and Transnational Politics, Routledge, New York.

Robertson, R (1995): Globalisation: Time Space and Homogeniety-heterogeniety In: M. Featherstone S. Lash and R. Robertson (eds) *Global Modernities*, Sage, London, pp. 25-44

Sen, A (1999): *Development as Freedom*, Oxford University Press, Oxford.

Sinha, Archana (2004): Micro Finance for Women's Empowerment, *Kurukshetra*, April, Vol. 52, No. 6.

Tripathy, K.K. (2004): Self-help Groups. A Catalyst of Rural Development, *Kurukshetra*, June, Vol. 52, No. 8.

Micro-finance
Reaching the Poor

Dr. Suman Kalyan Chaudhury*

Abstract

The prime function of micro-finance has to bringing access to financial services to the poor, to those who are neglected by the formal banking sector and it behaves as their social mission. Mainstream banks target clients that have collateral. The poor do not have assets to act as collateral, therefore they are ignored by the formal financial sector. These banks tend to be found in urban centres while the majority of the poor in the developing world live in rural areas, where financial services are not provided. Therefore, if MFIs are to fill this void they must reach out to the rural poor. Micro-finance plays a vital role in providing financial services to the poor people thus enabling them to utilize their entrepreneurial abilities to the fullest extent possible. Generally microfinance services fall under four mechanisms: *Loans, savings, insurance and pensions.* However,

* **Faculty Member, Alphia Institute of Business Management, Bhubaneswar.**

if MFIs are to meet their social mission of serving the poor, financial services need to reach the rural poor. *This article examines evidence from major impact studies on micro-finance to answer the question: Can Micro-finance reach very large number of the poor mass and remain sustainable to yield important impact?*

Micro-finance programmes have a potentially significant contribution to economic, social, political and psychological empowerment of the poor in general, women in particular. Through access to timely credit, savings, insurance and entrepreneurial training, women have become successful entrepreneurs, increased their household income and well-being. The banks and the SHGs by providing financial assistance, organizing skill-based training programmes in rural as well as semi-urban areas to preach the essence of developed economic development and its sustained contribution to the rural economy to dream a golden India ahead.

Preamble

The prime function of micro-finance has to bringing access to financial services to the poor, to those who are neglected by the formal banking sector and it behaves as their social mission. Mainstream banks target clients that have collateral. The poor do not have assets to act as collateral, therefore they are ignored by the formal financial sector. These banks tend to be found in urban centers while the majority of the poor in the developing world live in rural areas, where financial services are not provided. Therefore, if Micro-finance Institutions (MFIs) are to fill this void they must reach out to the rural poor. However, according to past studies, micro-finance is only reaching a small fraction of the estimated demand of the poor for financial services (Littlefield and Rosenberg, 2004). A major thrust in recent years for improving lives of womenfolk and alleviating rural poverty through the non-governmental organizations (NGOs) in India is promoting micro-finance through self-help groups (SHGs). The present scenario indicates that currently around 75 per cent of the credit supply is via the SHG-Bank linkage route largely financed by the National Bank for Agriculture and Rural Development (NABARD) and the rest comes from MFIs, increasingly backed by commercial banks. Micro-finance plays a vital role in providing financial services to the poor people thus enabling them to utilize their entrepreneurial abilities to the fullest extent possible. Generally micro-finance services fall under four mechanisms: *Loans, savings, Insurance & pensions.*

The MFIs do not have the depth of outreach that is needed to meet the demands of the rural poor. Micro-finance Institutions can provide one or a combination of services depending upon the objectives of their operation. Serving the rural poor in the developing world involves a major financial commitment, which is too expensive to run rural microfinance projects. Claessens (2005) states that high transaction costs, small volumes and the high costs of expanding outreach, make it unprofitable to serve the rural poor. It is for this reason that commercial banks are positioned to function in areas of high population density. However, if MFIs are to meet their social mission of serving the poor, financial services need to reach the rural poor.

Diverse Root

Modern micro-finance has roots in the cooperative movement dating from the nineteenth century, in the rural finance experience post-World War II and in the micro-enterprise development sector starting in the 1970s and these diverse roots intertwine with at least five common objectives:

(a) **Micro-enterprise Development:** by providing financial inputs and services to informal-sector entrepreneurs building their tiny business to the point of employing not just family members but others as well in the same locality.

(b) **Innovation/Investment Promotion:** by offering credit as both incentive and the enabler, for example, to small-scale farmers to adopt new inputs, practices and technologies to increase productivity of labour and land leading to more food production and/or farm income or more broadly in the population, to promote behavioural change for better health and nutrition.

(c) **Consumption-smoothing:** by providing poor families with relatively inexpensive credit and convenient savings services that effectively help the family have enough cash through the year to reduce the impact of the annual hungry season; major expenses, such as school fees or weddings and/or devastation of major economic shocks due to family illness, death of a bread-winner, loss of livestock or of crop, or natural disaster besides scanty rain might cause damage.

(d) **Women's Empowerment, and more generally build of Social Capital, to Support self-help** efforts at the family and community levels and to strengthen the voice of women and other marginalized groups as rights holders and agents of local development.

(e) **Financial Systems Development**, or financial sector deepening, both of which seek to lower the cost and increase the convenience of financial services so that the "unbanked" - even the very poor - can be reached by commercially viable enterprises.

All the above five objectives are important intermediate steps toward the international goal of poverty reduction. The wonderful feature of micro-finance is that it can achieve all of these objectives. That is, a single micro-finance product delivery system can satisfy most of these, and a combination of products and delivery systems can satisfy all of these objectives. However, micro-finance practitioners and supporters often differ in their ideas and motives; the order of priority they give to the common objectives may differ widely too.

The question is presented graphically in Fig 4.1, which shows the wealth pyramid popularized by C K Prahalad's text, *The Fortune at the Bottom of the Pyramid.* The number of people and their annual per capita expenditure are taken from VISA International & World Bank. The solid horizontal line approximates an international poverty line. The dashed lines below the poverty line correspond to 2 dollars-a-day and dollar-a-day expenditure per capita. Commercial banks have traditionally, and mostly still do, reach only the top of the pyramid. Credit unions, especially those based on community rather than workplace, have done better in reaching further down the pyramid through their cooperative principles and lower cost structures, but even they do not generally reach below the international poverty line. The innovations of micro-finance have made it commercially feasible to reach further down still, whether it be done by a specialized micro-finance institution (MFIs) or as a distinct line of service offered by a commercial bank or a credit union seeking to go down market. It is generally agreed that financially sustainable micro-finance operations reach the "near poor" and the "upper poor". Further down the pyramid, there is the question (symbolized by the dotted line arrows from "microfinance" on Fig. 4.1) about the sustainability and impact of micro-finance when offered to large number of the "poor" especially those living on the borderline of destitution; that is, those living on a dollar a day or less.

Exclusion of Women

Before 1990s, credit schemes exclusively for rural women as target groups were almost negligible. The concept

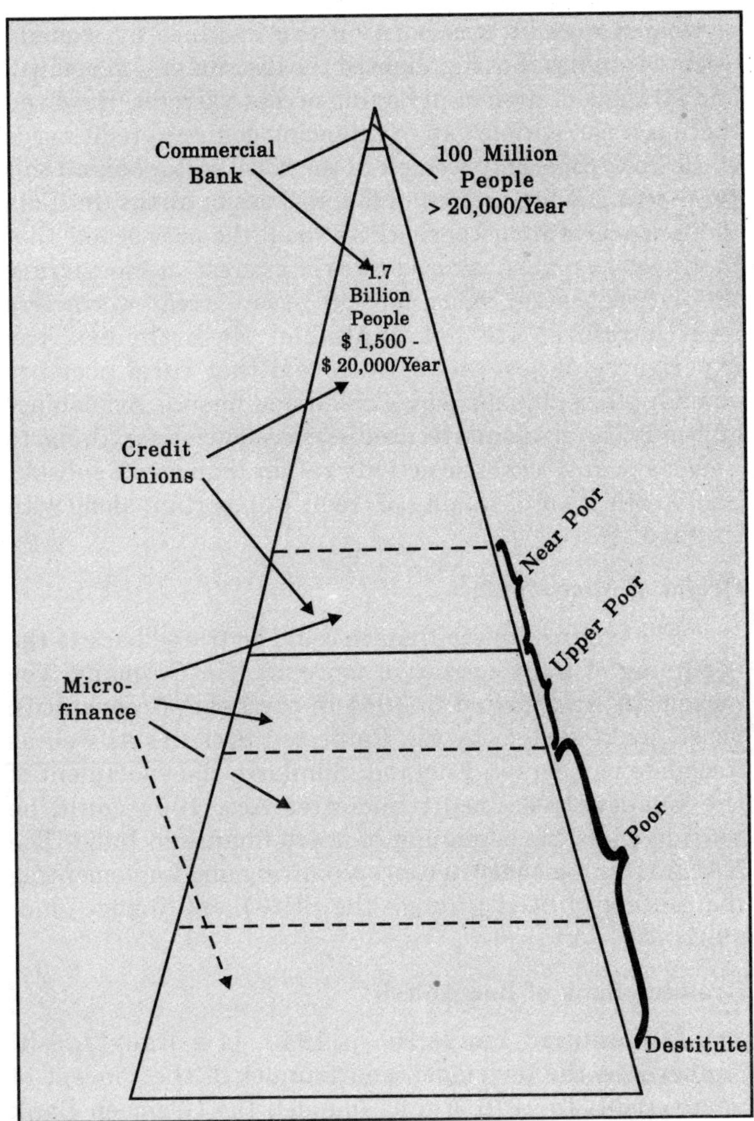

Fig. 4.1: Micro-finance can Reach the Lower Income Levels

Source: VISA International, World Bank, C.K. Prahalad

of women's credit was born on the instance by women-oriented studies that highlighted the discrimination against, and struggle of women in having access to credit. However, there is a perceptible gap in financing genuine credit needs of the poor, especially women in the rural sector behind this persistent gap lies certain unfounded assumptions. In India there are certain misconceptions about the poor people that they need loan at subsidized rates of interest on short terms; they lack education, skills, capacity to save, credit worthiness and therefore, are not bankable. Nevertheless, the experiences of several SHGs reveal that rural poor are actually efficient managers of credit and finance. Availability of timely and adequate credit is essential for them to undertake any economic activity rather than credit subsidy. Said in other words quality of credit is important along with its quantity.

Origin of Micro-finance

The origin of micro-finance could be traced back to the beginning of the cooperative movement in Germany. The movement was started in 1944 in the field of cooperative based credit system by the Raiffeisen Societies as well as Rochdale pioneers in England. Similarly, the enactment of the Cooperative Credit Societies Act, 1904 could be considered as the beginning of micro finance in India. The NABARD is a pioneer in conceptualizing and implementing the concept of SGH through the SHG-Bank linkage since 1992.

Grameen Bank of Bangladesh

Muhammad Yunus, born 1940, is a Bangladeshi banker and the developer and founder of the concept of micro-credit. In 1976, Yunus founded the Grameen Bank to make loans to poor Bangladeshis. Since then the Grameen Bank has issued more than three million dollar in loans to some 2.4 million borrowers. To ensure repayment, the bank uses a system of "solidarity groups". Small informal groups which apply together for loans and whose members act as co-guarantors of repayment and support one another's efforts at economic self-advancement. As it has grown, the Grameen Bank has also developed other systems of alternate credit that serve the poor. The success of the Grameen model has inspired similar efforts throughout the developing world and even in industrialized nations including the United States.

Micro-finance in India and Micro-enterprise

Micro-financing as another viable alternative approach to direct financing individual micro-enterprise came up very recently in India. The most favoured channel is the SHG-bank linkage programme where micro-entrepreneurship is indirectly financed by banks. Here neither bank takes up the individual borrower responsibility nor does bank exert pressure on them for timely recovery. It is the pure pressure of collective responsibility of the members of the SHG brings the principal and interest to bank in time.

Starting with a significant upward movement since the mid-90s, micro-finance through independent micro-finance institutions (MFIs) and through linking the self-help groups have played a commendable role. A study by the NABARD has found that 400 women join the self-help group over a whopping 22.50 lakh SHGs have so far been offered minimum banking service and NABARD expects to provide credit support to 5.85 lakh new groups by the year 2007 with 60 per cent of them coming from 13 under-developed States.

Considering a ratio of one-third of SHG members gone for any entrepreneurial activities and an average of 12 members per SHG (a conservative estimate), the achievement so far is commendable at national level. Till 2005 more than 64 lakhs of entrepreneurs have started their ventures either individually or collectively. The average loan size per member of SHG or per enterprise justifies the case of micro-financing (Table 4.1). No bank will like to give such a small loan to a large population. This in fact a

Table 4.1: Cumulative Progress of Self-help Groups Bank Linage Programme in India

(Rs. in Crore)

Year	No. of SHGs	Bank SHGs	Re-Finance by NABARD
1992-93	255	0.29	0.27
1993-94	620	0.65	0.46
1994-95	2,122	2.44	2.13
1995-96	4,757	6.06	5.66
1996-97	8,598 (3271)	11.84 (3982.76)	10.65 (3844)
1997-98	14,31.7	23.76	21.39
1998-99	32,995	57.07	52.06
1999-00	94,645	192.98	150.13
2000-01	1147759 (1234.90)	193.00 (1530.07)	150.10 (1309.39)
2001-02	263825	480.90	400.70
2002-03	463478	1026.30	796.50
2003-04	717360	2048.70	1418.80
2004-05	1079991 (840.96)	3904.20 (19922.90)	2124.20 (1315.19)
2005-06	1618476	6898.00	3092.00
2006-07	2238565	11398.00	4160.00
2007-08	29,24,973 (170.83)	18041.00 (362.09)	5459.00 (156.99)

Source: NABARD website.

Note: The percentages have been computed by assuming 1992-97, 1996-97, 2000-01, 2004-05 as the base years.

transformation in the rural society and would contribute to the overall utilization of entrepreneurial talents. Considering the vast rural population of this country and the growth rate of micro-finance, it can be well assumed that if this pace continues in future there will be a big metamorphosis in rural society. It seems that micro-financing is going to be the sole determinant of micro-enterprise development in India.

Pivotal Role of NABARD

The NABARD established as an apex institution, accredited with all matters concerning policy, planning and operations in the field of credit for agriculture and other economic activities in rural India with a vision to facilitate sustained access to financial services for the unreached poor in rural areas through various micro-finance innovations in a cost effective and sustained manner. The NABARD has been working as a catalyst in promoting and linking more and more SHGs to the banking system. The pioneering efforts at this direction were made by NABARD in 1991-92, pilot project for linking about 500 SHGs with banks was launched by NABARD in consultation with R.B.I. It is considered as a landmark development in banking for the poor. Further it was decided that NABARD would continue to provide refinance to banks under the linkage project at the rates stipulated from time to time.

Role of Self-help Groups

The SHGs of rural women consists of members who are the poor, having low saving capacity and who depend on money-lenders for meeting their consumption needs and social obligations. Formation of women into self-help groups paved a way to develop their socio-economic standards, thereby building self-confidence. Women in SHGs have been encouraged by the government as well as NGOs to undertake self-employment ventures with locally available resources. The SHGs are of recent origin in rural India for helping more than 17 million women from villages improve their incomes. The SHGs have also helped women campaign against oppressive social practices and become a force of development in their villages. Before 1990s, credit schemes for rural women were almost negligible. The concept of women's credit was born on the insistence by women-oriented studies that highlighted the discrimination and struggle of women in having access to credit.

Micro-finance and Poverty Alleviation

Poverty alleviation has been one of the key development challenges over the decades. One of the identified key constraints facing by the poor is lack of access to formal sector credit. It will facilitate them to take advantage of economic opportunities to increase their level of output, hence move out of poverty. Credit is considered to be an essential input to increase productivity, mainly land and labour. It is believed that credit boots income levels, increases employment at the household level and thereby alleviates poverty. Credit facilitates poor people to triumph over their liquidity constraints and undertake some income generating activities. Furthermore, credit helps poor people to smoothen their consumption patterns in times of lean periods of the year (Binswanger and Khandker, 1995). The improved consumption is an investment in the productivity of the labour force or human capital. Hence, credit will maintain the productive capacity of rural poor households (Heidhues, 1995; Hulme and Mosely, 1996; Mosely and Hulme, 1998; Hulme, 2000; Navajas *et al.*, 2000). The proposed goal of micro-finance sector is to improve the welfare of the poor as a result of better access to small loans. The lack of access to credit for the poor may have negative consequences for various household level outcomes including technology adoption, agricultural productivity, food security, nutrition, health and overall welfare. Access to credit therefore affects welfare outcomes by alleviating the capital constraints of poor households. Access to credit in addition increase the poor households' risk-bearing ability, improves their risk-copying strategies and enables consumption smoothing over time. By so doing, microfinance is argued to improve the welfare of the poor (Navajas, *et al.*, 2000; Diagne and Zellar, 2001).

Micro-finance programmes have a potentially significant contribution to economic, social, political and psychological empowerment of the poor in general, women in particular. Through access to timely credit, savings, insurance and entrepreneurial training, women have become successful entrepreneurs, increased their household income and well-being. Regardless of their scale, outreach, location and the type of clients, all microfinance programme intervention target one thing in common-human development that is geared towards both the economic and social upliftment of the people that they cater for.

SHGs-Bank Linkage Programme

The SHGs-Bank linkage programme in India is the largest micro-finance programme in the world. The NABARD has been playing supportive role by way of refinancing banks, organizing training programmes for NGOs, bank officers and SHG members for upgrading skills for smooth operation of SHGs-Bank linkage. The launching of pilot project initiating the SHG-Bank linkage in February, 1992 is indeed a landmark development in banking with the poor as it has been covering poorest of the poor who were so far been neglected by the formal financial sector. The number of credit linked SHGs, bank loan disbursement and refinance by NABARD has posted a substantial growth by 327 per cent, 3983 per cent and 3844 per cent by SHGs banks and NABARD respectively during 1996-97 over the respective figures in 1992-93 (Table 4.1).

Conclusion

Micro-finance programme has a significant role to play in Indian economy for boosting micro entrepreneurial activities for creating productive assets coupled with employment generation. So, in order to cover all the poor households, particularly BPL households, there is need for providing full support by the government, financial institutions and NGOs to SHGs programme. So far the

SHGs-bank linkage programme has been much successful in achieving quantitative targets and qualitative output. The need of the hour is to make the programme more qualitative, that is, enriching the lives of poorest of the poor in the context of globalised developed socio-economic environment. Political interference in the functioning of Self- Help Groups should be avoided and kept away from the scenario. Around 90 per cent of the aggregate groups are women self-help groups. These groups have to face problems such as, indifferent attitude of bank officers, exploitation by promoting NGOs, lack of marketing facilities for product/services. These bottlenecks should be rooted out on priority basis. Women groups should be given responsibility of running Anganwadi, fair price shops so that they become a permanent entities and mentors. The banks and the SHGs by providing financial assistance, organizing skill based training programmees in rural as well as semi urban areas to preach the essence of developed economic development and its sustained contribution to the rural economy to dream a golden India ahead.

REFERENCES

Armendariz de Aghion, B and Morduch. *The Economics of Micro-finance.* The MIT Press: Cambridge, MA, 2005.

Basu, Priya (2006), *Improving Access to Finance for India's Rural Poor,* The World Bank: Washington, D.C.

Diagne, A. and M. Zellar (2001), *Access to Credit and Its Impact in Malawi,* Research Report No. 116 Washington, D.C., USA; International Food Policy Research Institute (IFPRI).

Edgcomb, E. and Barton, L. (1998), Social Intermediation and Micro-finance Programmes: A Literature Review, Micro-enterprise Best Practices, USAID.

Goetz, A.M. and Sen Gupta, R. (1994), Who Takes the Credit? Gender, Power and Control Over Loan use in Rural Credit Programmes in Bangladesh, *World Development,* 24 (1): 45-63.

Hashemi, S.M., Schuler, S.R and Riley, A.P. (1996), Rural Credit Programmes and Womens'Empowerment in Bangladesh, *World Development,* 24(4): 635-653.

Heidhues, F. (1995), Rural Finance Markets: An Important Tool to Fight Against Poverty, *Quarterly Journal of International Agriculture*, 34 (2): 105-108.

Hossain, M. (1988). *Credit for Alleviation of Rural Poverty: The Grameen Bank in Bangladesh*, Washington DC: IFPRI

Hulme, David (2000), Impact Assessment Methodologies for Microfinance: Theory, Experience and Better Practices, *World Development*, 28(1): 79-98.

Hulme, David and Paul Mosley (1996), *Finance Against Poverty*. Vols. 1 and 2. London and New York: Routledge.

Jeromi, P.D. (2006), Financial Inclusion: Regional Perspective, Paper Presented in the National Conference on Financial Inclusion and Beyond Issues and Opportunities for India, Cochin, India (19-20 September, 2006).

Khandker, S.R. (1998) *Fighting Poverty with Micro-credit Experience in Bangladesh*, Published for the World Bank, Oxford University Press.

Littlefield, E, Morduch, J, and Hashemi, S. (2003), Is Micro-finance as Effective Strategy to Reach the Millennium Development Goals, CGAP, *Focus Note*, 24.

Marie, Godquin (2004), Micro-finance Repayment Performance in Bangladesh: How to Improve the Allocation of Loans by MFIs, *World Development*, 32 (11): 1909-1926.

McKernan, Signe-Mary (2002), The Impact of Micro-credit Programmes on Self-employment Profits: DO Non-credit Programme Aspects Matter, *The Review of Economics and Statistics*, 84 (1): 93-115.

Morduch, J. (1999), The Micro Finance Promise, *Journal of Economic Literature*, 37 (4): 1569-1614.

Mosely, Paul (2001), Micro-finance and Poverty in Bolivia, *The Journal of Development Studies*, 37: 101-132.

Mosely, Paul and David Hulme (1998), Micro Enterprise Finance: Is There a Conflict Between Growth and Poverty Alleviation? World Development 26: 783-790.

Schreiner, M. "*Aspects of Outreach: A Framework for the Discussion.*

Sebstad, J and M Cohen. *Micro-finance, Risk Management and Poverty*. USAID - AIMS. 2000.

5

Micro-credit and Self-help Groups in Rural Development

Dr. B. Eswar Rao Patnaik*
Dr. Sudhansu Sekhar Nayak**

Introduction

In the third world countries, including India with a high degree of rural population an institution is necessary at the central level for looking into the financial needs' of the poor at the grass-root level, both belonging to urban and rural areas. A large proportion of rural population is socio-economically backward who want to take up productive activities, lack of resources and adequate credit affect their economic activities. So there is need of credit.

The micro-credit refers to the provision of financial services to lower income groups in rural, semi-urban and urban areas for enabling them to raise their income levels and improve living standards. Micro-credit Institutions (MCIs) provide loans for consumption, production activities or for small businesses. Of late, a range of financial services other than credit such as savings, micro-insurance etc., also

* Reader in Economics (Retd.), S.B.R.G. (Autonomous) Womens' College, Berhampur, Orissa.

** Sr. Faculty (Commerce), R.N. College, Dura, Berhampur, Orissa.

included under micro-finance. The characteristics of micro-finance are that the financial services is small in magnitude and those who avail the services are poor and very poor.

Need of Micro-finance

The importance of micro-finance lies in the fact that the formal institutional banking sector has not lived up to its social responsibility of meeting the financial needs of the poor duel to various reasons such as: (i) lack of adequate branch network in rural areas; (ii) the inability of the poor to offer satisfactory collaterals for the loans; and (iii) lack of education and awareness among the poor. This is in spite of the fact that India today has an extensive banking infrastructure. The credit requirement of the poor in India has been estimated to be around Rs. 50,000 crore per annum. Against this requirement the credit outstanding of the poor with the formal banking sector i.e. stated to be Rs. 5000 crores or ten per cent of the total demand. According to the sample survey conducted by world bank and NCAER in 2003, in Andhra Pradesh and Uttar Pradesh around 87 per cent of marginal farmers don't access credit from the formal banking sector. Most of the benefits of the so-called extensive banking infrastructure have to gone to relatively better off people, around 66 per cent of large farmers have a deposit account and 40 per cent have access credit.

Micro-finance Institutions

The past 15 years saw the entry of various types of Micro-finance Institutions in the rural credit sector. Most of these are based in the Grameen Bank Model of Bangladesh. This model has the solidarity groups at the base, each of which comprising five borrowers. Eight solidary groups constitute a "Centre". Ten centres a "Cluster" and seven clusters a branch. Several such branches constitute an Micro-financial Institutions. Micro Financial Institutions in India register themselves either as societies, trusts, non-banking financial companies or local area banks and are governed by their respective rules and regulations. In India. Micro-credit programme are implemented through group structures, which are known as self-help group.

Self-help Groups

A Self-help Group (SHG) is a registered or unregistered group of micro-entrepreneurs having homogenous social and economic background. They mutually agree to contribute to a common fund and to meet their emergency needs on mutual help basis. The group members use collective wisdom and peer pressure to ensure proper end use of credit and timely repayment. In fact, peer pressure has been recognized as an effective substitute for collaterals.

An economically poor individual gains strength as part of group. Besides financing through SHGs reduces transaction costs for both lenders and borrowers. While lenders have to handle only a single SHG account instead of a large number of small-sized individual accounts, borrowers as part of a SHG cut down expenses or travel to and from the branch and other places for completing paper work and on the loss of work days in canvassing for loans.

Role of SHGs

There has been rapid growth of self-help groups in the past one decade. The self-help groups play an important role in rural development. The SHGs growth which has almost assured the form of movement represents a massive grassroot level mobilisation of poor rural women in small informal associations capable of forging links with formal systems to help access financial and other services needed for their socio-economic development. Basically SHGs are being promoted as a part of the micro-finance interventions aimed at helping the poor to obtain easily financial services like saving, credit and insurance.

The promotion of SHGs in India began more formally, in 1992 with the launch of the SHG - Bank Linkage programme by National Bank for Agriculture and Rural Development (NABARD). The aim of the programme was to improve rural poor's access to formal credit system in the cost effective and sustainable manner by making use of SHGs.

A self-help group is a small and informal association of poor having perfectly similar socio-economic background and come together to realize some common goals based on principle of self-help and collective responsibility. The SHGs helps the poor to come together to pool their savings and access credit facilities. A SHG by tapping socio-capital like trust and reciprocation helps in replacing physical collateral, a major hurdle faced by the poor in obtaining formal credit. Then through the principles of joint liability and peer pressure, a SHG ensures prompt loan recovery from the members. In the process, a SHG helps the poor, especially women to establish their credit-worthiness.

The major role of SHGs is seen in terms of their potential to empower the women members. The participation in SHG and the access obtained to savings and credit can play a transformational role for women, socially and economically. The access to saving and credit helps a women member to contribute to her family's financial needs for consumption and production purpose. The ability to meet such needs of the family would enhance the standing of the women in the family leading to better gender relations. The continued participation in SHG is further likely to enhance the awareness skills and other abilities of the women resulting in building of individual self esteem and in getting due social recognition.

The self-help group programme is now more than a decade old. There is a need to explore:

1. the extent the SHGs have helped poor women to get access to saving and credit;

2. to what extent the improved access to financial capital has contributed towards attending goals like poverty alleviation and women's empowerment?; and

3. what are the challenges and constraints faced, by SHGs in playing their expected role?

According to some available studies it is indicated that as a result of participation in SHGs, members have been able to accumulate significant savings. In States such as Andhra Pradesh an average SHG member has accumulated individual savings up to Rs. 1,800. In mature SHGs the average individual savings have been as high as Rs. 10,000. Though in absolute amount the savings is small, it becomes significant when seen from the angle that bulk of the SHG members hail from poorer communities unable to save conveniently and safely earlier. Own savings can be handy and useful in many ways. Many SHGs members even consider development of the habit of savings as the major impact of their participation in SHGs. There are evidence to indicate that using the opportunity of savings provided by the SHGs, women are able to meet various socio-economic needs like housing, education and marriage.

In the recent past in Nagaland, some women managing a group responded to their own self-help group, which was registered on 20th April, 2006. Soon their group become active. They started holding meetings at least once in two weeks. They would all attend these meetings as the absentee would have to pay a fine of five rupees. Cooperative Education project officials helped them to learn more about income generating activities that they could undertake. They were trained in making woollen shoes. The training programme was conducted in collaboration with the Nagaland State Industries Department.

The group then not only started making woollen shoes and earned a steady income but also go beyond. Later the group was also trained in woollen carpet making. The other achievements of SHG was in making of banana chips, potato chips, preparing *papads* from sticky rice and making pickles, They have also mastered the art of stitching jute bags and other handicrafts.

This SHG now has a steady income of their own. Now they have no difficulty in contributing Rs. 50 per month to their fund as each member's monthly income at present ranges from Rs. 500 to 600. Their total savings have accumulated to over Rs. 40,000, not a mean considering that these very women at one time were in awe of talking to any official for help.

Impact on Poverty

A foremost discernible is the reduced dependence of SHG house holds on informal sources of credit. The members of the SHGs have been above to reduce their dependence on money-lender very significantly. A study of SHGs reported a decline in the share of money lenders loan from 66 to 15 per cent for the members. In another study, nearly 51 per cent of the members closed their old debt with the money-lenders using SHG loans. The members at the same time have been able to generate a substantial surplus for themselves due to cheaper interest paid on loans.

Through credit obtained from SHGs, the members have made efforts both to protect their families from various vulnerabilities as well as build their economic base to escape from poverty. This is evident from the fact that members are making use of SHG loans for diverse purposes. While use of loan for consumption purpose still remains a major item of utilisation, members are increasingly using the SHG loans for social and productive needs. Health, education and housing are some of the areas members have begun to increasingly channelise their loans. In Tamil Nadu it was found that nearly 14 per cent loan has been used lor housing purpose. In Andhra Pradesh it was found that nearly six per cent of members had utilised their loans for children education.

The SHG members are also using quite significantly SHG loans for regular economic activities like animal husbandry. The agriculture and petty business. This is evident from the fact that nearly 74 per cent of SHG members in Tamil Nadu have invested in creating various assets like land, livestock and household durables after joining SHGs. A study concluded that micro-finance seems to have played a more critical role in facilitating clients to cope with situations rather than deal with life-cycle events in sustainable manner.

Though SHGs have began to contribute in improving the economic conditions of the poor households, the impact does not seem to be a uniform phenomenon throughout. At the same time, there is no evident to establish the fact that the positive impact noticed in some instances are attributable to women's involvement. A study found that women have certainly become more visible as micro-finance clients, but being a client does not translate automatically in empowerment. The study found only mixed evidence about the role of micro-finance in either increasing women's awareness, mobility and skill development or enhance women's status in the household as income contributors and decision makers.

Self-help Group-Bank Cumulative

Micro-credit is a novel approach to banking with the poor. This approach in Bangladesh, bank credit is extended to the poor through Self-Help Groups, NGOs, credit unions etc. Micro-credit attempts to combine lower transaction costs and high degree of repayments. This is essential because of the involvement of potential beneficiaries of rural credit in the credit delivery system. The SHG - bank linkage programme, introduced and encouraged by NABARD in India, is now being implemented vigorously by more than 30,000 branches of commercial banks, RRBs and co-operative banks in 1999 over 520 districts in 30 States and Union Territories.

At the end of March, 2004 as many as 10.8 lakh SHGs are now linked with banks and 28,00 with NGOs. It is estimated that at the end of March 2004.

17 million very poor families will be brought within the fold of formal banking services, with 90 per cent women groups, having 95 per cent repayment performance with average loan. As per SHG and per family coming to Rs. 30,000 and Rs. 1,770 respectively. The cumulative loan disbursement towards SHG will come to Rs. 3,900 crore.

Conclusion

Micro-finance is the key *mantra* for a sustained and long term economic growth for India. It is a sharper focus today with the government taking keen interest to ensure a comprehensive and visible uplift of rural people through effective implementation of various schemes. It is clear that micro-finance is most important factor to attain sustainable rural development. There is a massive mobilization of women taking part in the SHG movement. The SHG movement has a good potential to help develop the socio-economic status of the rural poor and contribute towards women's emancipation.

REFERENCES

Anand, V.V., Micro-finance for Rural Development, *Yojana,* 52 (17): 63-64.

Indian Economy, Dan, R. & K.P.M. Sundaram, pp. 594-595.

Kainth, G.S. Innovation in Rural Financial System, *Kurukshetra,* 55 (6): 26-30.

Mishra, S.K. and Puri V.K. *Indian Economy,* 22 Edition pp. 347-348.

Mukherjee, Dhurjati, Relevance of Micro Credit: Bangladesh Example, *Kurukshetra,* 55(3): 31-32.

Sood, Archna, March of a Women's in Kohima to Success, *Kurukshetra,* Vol. 56, No. 1, pp. 43-44.

Shylendra, H.S. Role of Self-help Groups, *Yojana,* 52(6): 25-28.

6

SHGs Movement
Micro-finance Programme under Swarnajayanti Gram Swarozgar Yojana

Prabin Kumar Padhy*

Introduction

The contribution of the primary sector to India's Gross Domestic Product (GDP) has declined from 56.2 per cent in 1951-52 to 17.5 per cent in 2007-08. Despite this, the primary sector still provides livelihood support to about half of the country's rural and poverty-stricken population primarily engaged in farming on small land holdings and allied activities. The key problem of those dependent on agriculture, especially the poor, small and marginal farmers and weaker sections of the society, is non-availability of credit at reasonable and affordable rates of interest.

Finance is an important input of agriculture. In spite of notable expansion of bank branches and increased credit flow in the last few years, the overall higher order credit growth in the banking system has not supported the desired expansion of agricultural credit and credit to small scale industries sector. Table 6.1 shows the distribution of rural

* **Head, Deptt. of Business Administration, Gayatri Institute of Science & Technology, Berhampur, Ganjam, Orissa.**

Table 6.1: Distribution of Rural Population and Bank Offices in India

Year	Rural Population (in 000)	% of Rural Population to Total Population	Bank Offices Rural	Bank Offices Total	% of Rural Banks to Total Banks	Bank Office Per Rural Population
1971	3,29,932	75.1	4,817	13,622	35.4	0.068
1981	3,64,404	69.6	17,656	35,707	49.4	0.021
1991	4,11,281	65.4	35,206	60,220	58.5	0.012
2001	7,42,490	72.2	32,562	65,919	49.4	0.023
2002	7,52,506	72.0	32,380	66,190	48.9	0.023
2003	7,62,345	71.8	32,303	66,535	48.6	0.024
2004	7,72,006	71.5	32,121	67,188	47.8	0.024
2005	7,81,488	71.3	32,082	68,355	46.9	0.024
2006	7,90,786	71.1	30,750	69,118	44.5	0.026
2007	8,03,596	70.0	30,585	72,165	42.4	0.026

Source: Compiled from Handbook of Statistics on the Indian Economy (RBI) 2005-06 & 2007-08, *Census Statistics*, 1971, 1981, 1991, 2001 & *Population Projection Report of National Population Commission* (Gol), May, 2006.

population and rural bank offices in India from 1971. There were 4817 rural bank branches during 1971 catering to about 33 crores of people. The corresponding figures for 2007 were 30,585 and 80 crores respectively. In 1971, there were 0.068 Bank Offices for every person living in rural areas. This figure decelerated to 0.012 in 1991, the year which marks the beginning of the reforms and opening up of the Indian economy. After 1991, this indicator showed an increment to 0.023 in 2001 and 0.026 in 2007. Further, the percentage of rural bank offices to total bank offices was the highest (58.5%) at the end of 1991 and it gradually reduced to 42.4 per cent in 2007.

To reduce the rural-urban gaps the focus of the government has been on co-operative movements, priority sector lending and the operation, supervision, and monitoring of rural credit by designated rural financial agencies for the smooth, adequate and timely flow of credit to the rural people. However, due to low productivity and almost negative return in agriculture farmers are in search of other cost effective livelihood opportunities in the local areas concerned. The critical issue here is the financial inclusion of the farmers as they do not possess any valuable productive assets.

The traditional concern about non-accessibility of credit to the needy rural inhabitants is still alive. Although, the government banks have been offering credit at reasonable and affordable rates of interest, the major problems faced by the rural poor in accessing timely credit relate to loan documentation, collateral security, and general indifferent attitudes of the bank officials. It is noted that on all India basis 41 per cent of the population is unbanked. The coverage is rural areas is 39 per cent as against 60 per cent in the urban areas. With the disappointing result of these formal financial agencies, the country has now started relying on an innovative model of informal credit delivery mechanism, popularly known as micro-finance. Micro-finance and Micro-credit. The word micro-finance is provision of credit and other financial services and products of very small amounts to the poor in rural, semi-urban and urban areas for enabling the members to raise the level of income and improve their standard of living. So, anyone availing micro-finance has to engage in some productive activities that will generate some income. Whereas micro-credit caters to the commercial needs of poor for enabling them to raise their income level and to improve the standard of living. Micro-finance is also treated as an effective employment generator in rural areas having the capability to sustain income of the households by ensuring them opportunity at work.

The Government of India's Micro-finance and self-employment Programme called Swarnajayanti Gram Swarozgar Yojana (SGSY) is based on the principle of financial inclusion and aims at poverty alleviation by providing hassle free credit services to the Below Poverty Line (BPL) people. This programme draws its essence from self-help group (SHG) - Bank linkages in rural India and has been built around the basic psychological principle of human nature which rests on the feeling of self-worth and the important feature of self-help.

Objectives

- To review the nature and functions of SHGs and examine the suitability of government directed micro-finance activities as a compliment to the formal credit delivery mechanism of the nationalized banks, and scheduled banks.
- To analyze the impact of Swarnajayanti Gram Swarojagar Yojana Programme intervention to employment generation and income.

Genesis of SHG Movement

The genesis of SHGs in the world economy can be traced to the birth of Grameen Bank in Bangladesh in

1975-76, when the Nobel laureate Prof. Md. Yunus started lending $27 to 42 people in a village (Jobra) near Chittagong University, where he was teaching.

The launching of the pilot phase of the SHG-Bank linkage programme with 255 SHGs in February, 1992 could be considered as a landmark development in banking with the poor in India. At present 34,77,965 SHGs are working under different promotional institutional in India. The SHGs comprise 53 Lakhs of members, out of which 90 per cent of them are women. Generally, the economic position of women is adversely affected by their lack of access to productive sources. As economic position directly affects her bargaining position and power in the family as well as in the society. Weak economic position also adversely affects the ability of women to act against social violence, social evils etc. Almost all low income women are neglected by the people in the society. So, the women should get access to finance and economic participation which will help them to gather confidence and capacity to use their voice. Financial freedom also increases the status of women in the society and enables them to generate income. Women's access to savings and credit gives them a greater economic role in decision making and optimize their own and household's welfare.

- In 1992, NABARD launched a pilot project to form self-help groups and provided bank finance to them.
- In November 1994, RBI constituted a working group on "Non-Government Organization and self-help group" under the chairmanship of Shri S.K. Kalia the then M.D, NABARD.
- As per the recommendations of the group, RBI asked banks vide its circular dated 2nd April, 1996 to provide finance to SHGs as a normal banking activities.
- In 1999-2000, Government of India wanted to give a boost to SHG concept.

Data and Methodology

The study is based on the Secondary Data collected from Leading Magazines, Journals, Articles, Seminar Publications and leading newspapers reports for ten years i.e 1999-2000 to 2008-09. The progress of Self-Help Groups in India as well as Orissa under SGSY have been tabulated, analyzed and studied.

Structure of the Study

The study on SHGs their physical and financial progress in India as well as Orissa with SGSY programme has been divided into Eight Sections. viz. 1st section deals with objectives. the 2nd section includes the details and genesis of SHGs, 3rd section contains the Data and Methodology, 4th section contains Concepts, features of SHGs, 5th section deals with review of literature. 6th section contains Role of NABARD and criteria of bank finance to SHGs, 7th section includes Physical and Financial Progress in India as well as Orissa under SGSY programme.8th section includes the concluding part.

Concepts of Self-help Groups

The growth of self-help groups as a powerful tool for empowering women at country level is the result of NABARD's work for promoting 500 self-help groups in India. Following the success of the project, the Reserve Bank of India has issued directives to Banks in 1996 to cover Self-Help Groups as a mainstream activity under priority sector lending portfolio.

Self-help Groups are one of the micro-finance institutions in the field of economic development. According to Marguerite S. Robinson "Micro-finance refers to small scale financial services for both credits and deposits, that are provided to people who farm or fish or herd, operate small or micro enterprise where goods are produced, recycled, repaired, or traded, provided services, work for wages or commissions, gain income from renting out small amount of land, vehicles, draft animals, or machinery and tools and to other individuals and local groups in developing countries in both rural and urban area."

Indian micro-finance institutions are following different models in micro-finance delivery based on their clients, focus area, interest rate, savings linkages, collateral, coverage, and organizational structure. The models can be classified under four approaches namely:

1. SHG Group/Promotion Approach
2. Micro Finance Institution Approach
3. Micro Enterprise Development Approach
4. Social Development Approach.

SHGs/Group Promotion Approach

It is based on the promise that NGOs, MFIs promote groups and provide those services in small scale to the rural entrepreneurs, women entrepreneurs, artisans craftsmen on easy credit basis.

Professor Yunus observes its mission to help poor people to help themselves to overcome poverty. It is not based on any collateral security. It is initiated as a challenge to conventional banking which rejected poor as non credit worthy.

Features of Self-help Groups

- SHGs are group of persons having similar social and economic background of small means
- SHGs may be registered or unregistered consisting of 10-20 members
- The groups conduct meeting at regular intervals pertaining to collection of savings by members and lending of funds to needy members for production and consumption purposes.

- Out of this fund, the members are given credit as per term decided by the group.
- The amount of loan procedure is simple and flexible, carrying low rates of interest on small amount of loans.
- SHGs borrow from banks or voluntary agencies to lend to its members.
- NGOs may help SHGs in procuring raw materials and marketing of the produce.
- SHGs maintain records such as:
  - *(i)* Membership Register;
  - *(ii)* Minute Book;
  - *(iii)* Loan Disbursed Book;
  - *(iv)* Savings Deposit Book;
  - *(v)* Quorum.
- SHGs can have one Savings Bank account operated through some of their Authorized Signatories to withdraw the amounts from the bank for the purpose of needy members.
- SHGs can elect from among themselves a leader and sub leader to manage group and activities.

Review of Literature

Puhazhendi, V. and Badtya, K.C (2002): have made an attempt to study the impact of micro finance channelised through SHG Bank linkage programme for the poor. The socio economic condition in pre and post SHG were compared. The study finding concluded that SHG contributed significantly to the social and economic improvement of members.

Anushree Sinha (2008): has made an attempt to study the impact and sustainability of SHG-Bank Linkage on the socio economic condition of the members in pre and post SHG scenario.

Dr. B.Eswar Rao Patnaik and **Mr. Rajesh Pashu Palak:** They have analyzed the role of RRBs in accelerating the development of SHG groups.

Role of NABARD in Relation to the Functioning of SHGs

- NABARD launched the project in 1992 to provide finance to SHGs.
- NABARD provides resources and training to NGOs for the formation of SHGs.
- NABARD provides training to Bank officials on formation of SHGs and closely monitors the progress of RRBs, Co-operative Banks.
- NABARD provides root level training programme for strengthening the SHGs.
- NABARD provides refinance facilities to banks to the extent of 100 per cent against their lending to SHGs on very concessional rates of interest. The banks are free to charge any rates of interest suitable to them, preferably lower.

Criteria of Bank Finance for Self-help Groups

- The size of SHGs should be consisting of (10-20) members.
- The SHGs should have existed for at least six months.
- Financing to Self-Help Groups should be by Commercial Banks, Regional Rural Banks (RRBs), and Co-operative Banks.
- Advances to SHGs will be considered as a priority sector advance.
- SHGs can deal with any other area not coming under the jurisdiction of the Bank or branch of the Bank.
- Reserve Bank of India and NABARD has prescribed model documents to be complied with for the sanctioning of finance.

- Self-Help Groups should have a good track record.
- The maintain of accounts by SHGs should be audited.

Physical and Financial Progress of Self-help Groups in India from 1999-2000 to 2008-09

An analysis of the trend of SHGs formation under Swarnajayanti Gram Swarozgar Yojana between 1999-2000 and 2007-08 in the country indicates that the annual growth rate of formation of SHGs has not shown any definite increasing or decreasing trend over the years from 1999-2000 and 2007-08. Table 6.2 shows the number of SHGs assisted increased more than six fold from 29,017 in 1999-2000 to 1,81,386 during 2007-08. The number of SHGs assisted as a percentage of number of Self-Help Groups formed increased from a mere 9.9 per cent in 1999-2000 to about 59.1 per cent during 2007-08.As on October 1, 2008 7.06 Lakhs of SHGs had been linked with credit and had taken up economic activities.

Table 6.2 displays that an amount of Rs. 15,632 crore per annum is mobilized as credit and Rs. 7,630 crores towards subsidy disbursement during the past 10 years under the programme. This means the Credit: Subsidy ratio is only 2:1, which is well below the government norm of at least 3:1 (Ministry of Rural Development, 1999).The average per capita investment has been estimated to be Rs. 23,040 only. This was below the desired level of the Government's indicative and targeted per capita investment of Rs. 25,000 per beneficiaries (Ministry of Rural Development, 2007)

Physical and Financial Progress: Orissa

Table 6.3 indicates the financial and physical progress under Swarnajayanti Gram Swarojagar Yojana in Orissa since the inception of the programme. Up to 2008-09 out of 1.87 lakhs SHGs formed in the State of Orissa, only 34,943

Table 6.2: Physical and Financial Progress under SGSY since inception of Programmes 999-2008

Year	SHGs formed (Nos.)	SHGs Taken up Economic Activities (Nos.)	SHGs formed To Economic Activation (%)	Total Credit Mobilized Rs. (In Crores)	Total Subsidy Disbursed Rs. (In Crores)	Credit Subsidy Ratio	Per Capita Investment (Rs.)
1999-2000	2,92,426	29,017	9.9	1,056.50	541.7	2.0	17,113
2000-01	2,23,265	26,317	11.8	1,459.40	701.9	2.1	21,480
2001-02	4,34,387	30,576	7	1,329.70	665.6	2.0	21,283
2002-03	3,98,873	35,525	8.9	1,184.30	605.9	2.0	21,665
2003-04	3,92,136	50,717	12.9	1,302.10	713.4	1.8	22,471
2004-05	2,66,230	68,102	25.6	1658.20	858.8	1.9	22,555
2005-06	2,76,414	80,130	29	1,823.20	904.8	2.0	23,698
2006-07	2,46,309	1,37,931	56	2,291.20	971.1	2.4	19,281
2007-08	3,06,688	1,81,386	59.1	2,760.30	1,289.10	2.1	28,764
2008-09	1,10,015	66,952	60.9	767	378.2	2.0	32,093
Total/ Average	**29,46,743**	**7,06,653**	**24**	**15,631.80**	**7,630.40**	**2.0**	**23,040**

Source: Monitoring Division, Ministry of Rural Development, Gol.
Data compiled up to October 2008.

(i.e. 18.6%) had been credit linked and had taken up economic activities. The total subsidy disbursed is to the tune of Rs. 500 crores and total credit mobilized under the programme is Rs. 971 crores during 1999-2008. Such a huge investment under the programme has been made. However, this programme has not been successful in enhancing the per capita investment level appreciably. However, from Table 6.2 and Table 6.3, it is noticed that Orissa has witnessed a higher per capita investment i.e Rs. 23,893 as against the All-India Level of Rs. 23,040. This may be ascribed to the fact that a fund flow under the Swarnajayanti Gram Swarojagar Yojana is linked to the poverty incidence in a State. Orissa, one of the most backward States of the country, draws relatively higher proportion of subsidy than the other States. The credit subsidy ratio which is 1.9 shows the indifferent attitude of the banks in disbursing the matching credit to subsidy in higher doses.

Table 6.3 also indicates that while annual growth of SHGs formation between the years 2000-01 and 2007-08 have not been consistent, the SHGs linked to self-employment economic ventures followed a positive trend. The compound annual growth rate of SHGs formation and their linkage with economic activities between 1999-2000 and 2007-08 for all India was 0.6 per cent and 25.7 per cent, respectively. For Orissa, the same was 5.9 per cent and 33.8 per cent. This shows that in both the formation of SHGs and their linkage activities have a higher growth rate in Orissa.

As far as the State of Orissa is concerned it has become an ideal state for micro-financing. Recently, more than Rs. 250 crores has been financed through 25 micro-finance Institutions, The State's share comes around 0.85 per cent. The report clearly indicates that NABARD and SIDBI failed to deliver products and services in Orissa.

Table 6.3: Physical and Financial Progress under SGSY in Orissa since inception of Programmes 1999-2008

Year	SHGs Formed (Nos.)	SHGs Taken Up Economic Activities	SHGs Formed to Economic Activities on (%)	Total Credit Mobilized (Crores)	Total Subsidy Disbursed (Crores)	Credit Subsidy ratio	Per Capita Investment (Rs.)
1999-2000	10,334	1,011	9.8	94.17	50.38	1.9	19,369.70
2000-01	18,706	1,169	6.2	123.33	66.27	1.9	22,004.30
2001-02	31,732	1,296	4.1	82.63	46.99	1.8	21,885.40
2002-03	26,465	1,454	5.5	68.88	40.68	1.7	22395.60
2003-04	19,900	3,514	18.5	77.89	34.31	2.3	18925.70
2004-05	26,393	5,058	19.2	97.50	59.40	1.6	23878.00
2005-06	18,741	5,293	28.2	106.97	59.48	1.8	26047.70
2006-07	16,032	5,647	35.2	140.06	62.20	2.3	29,447.70
2007-08	16,403,	10,404	63.4	177.38	78.56	2.3	29,362.20
2008-09	3,403	97	2.9	2.51	1.27	2.0	25,610.90
Total/Average	1,87,209	34,943	18.7	971.38	499.58	1.9	23,892.70

Source: Monitoring Division of Ministry of Rural Development, Government of India. Data collected and compiled up to October, 2008.

Chief Minister of Orissa Naveen Patnaik had decided to replicate the Nobel laureate Prof. Mohd. Yunus's successful micro-credit model to strengthen women SHGs in the State after taking stock of the SHG movement in Orissa christened as Mission SHAKTI.

Mission SHAKTI, is a special and significant vehicle for economic development of the women, and self-employment generation in some pockets of Orissa. Similarly, another micro-finance institution RUDSETI also contributes in rural development and self-employment generation, by imparting training and developing the skill of entrepreneurs.

Table 6.4: Summary Statistics of SGSY in Indian during 1999-2008

1.	Self-help Groups formed (Nos.)	29,46,743
2.	Women SHG (per cent)	81.7
3.	SHGs Graded for financial package (per cent)	97.4
4.	SHGs Assisted to Graded (per cent)	24.6
5.	Total cumulative Funds available under SGSY (Rs. crores)	1610.7
6.	Subsidy disbursed (Rs. crore)	7630.4
7.	Total Credit mobilized (Rs. crores)	15,631.8
8.	Credit Subsidy Ratio	2.041
9.	Per Capita Investment (Rs.)	23,041
10.	Credit per SHG assisted (Rs.)	2,21,209

Source: Kurukshetra, January 2010.

A Decade of SGSY

An analysis of statistics on the progress of SGSY implementation in India between 1999-2000 to 2007-08 indicates that there are 29.46 lakhs of SHGs formed under SGSY out of which 81.7 per cent are exclusive women groups. 97.4 per cent of total SHGs formed were evaluated and formed suitable for financial linkage. Out of total SHGs, evaluated for financial linkage only 24.6 per cent were finaly assisted till March 2008. During 1999-2008 a cumulative sum of 15,631.8 crores of credit was mobilized against a subsidy of Rs. 7630.4 crores. This indicates a subsidy ratio of 2.04:1 against the government norm of 3:1. The per capita investment achieved was Rs. 23,041 against the target of Rs. 25,000. Out of the total amount disbursed, to the assisted beneficiaries, on an average one SHG got Rs. 2.21 Lakhs.

Conclusion

- The success of the rural micro-finance lies in the formation of quality groups, adequate and timely credit support along with the identification of appropriate and profitable economic activities.
- The credit to subsidy ratio under the programme has to be at least 3:1. Field level studies indicate a lot more is required by way of coordination among the different tiers of implementing agencies,viz bankers, government officials,
- The inbuilt coordination and monitoring mechanism within the programme has to be reviewed and redesigned ensuring the active involvement of programme implementing agencies.
- The selection of activities in a particular area should be determined by the availability of physical resources, skill and aptitude of the people and the market demand.
- For optimum forward and backward linkages the number of key economic activities should not exceed five.
- Micro-finance activities could help to improve the socio economic condition of the poor by addressing certain

issues relevant to income generation and capability enhancement. In Orissa self-help groups partici-pation can help protect the poor, particularly the women against poverty, insecurity, and social exclusion.

- Participatory decision making while mapping the local resources, identifying and selecting the economic activities.
- Last but not the least the absorption and repayment capacity of the members should determine the amount of financial support to be extended to them. Consumption loans should be definitely discouraged. Before extending any loan, even for productive purposes, an assessment by the group in consultation with all the programme implementing authorities must be made.

REFERENCES

Conference Souvenir of the 92nd Indian Economic Association, 2009, pp. 46-53.

Conference Volume Part-II of the 92nd Indian Economic Association, 2009 pp. 217-219.

Kurukshetra, July, 2005, pp. 43, January-2006, p. 37.

Misra, R.N. and G. Chandrayya Micro-finance for Agricultural Development, pp. 104-109.

Orissa Journal of Commerce. Vol. 29, January 2008 pp. 119, 188-192.

7

Role of United Artists Association for promoting Livelihood Strategy among the Marine Fishing Community in Orissa

Dr. Radha Krushna Panda*

Background

Recent empirical studies suggest that the number of people depending on full-time fishing in the coastal districts and regions have started to stagnate and even declining owing to the unfavourable external business environment. Few of the prominent studies also do indicate that in some countries and regions, occupational mobility and attractive alternative employment opportunities have diverted resources from the marine fishing to other non-fishing sectors (Tietze, 1985). Still Fisheries related activities provide important sources of livelihood for nearly seven million people in India (Government of India 2000). A livelihood comprises the capabilities, assets (including both material and social resources) and activities required for a means of living. A livelihood is said to be sustainable when

* **Faculty in Economics and Quantitative Methods, Indian Institute of Professional Studies (IIPS), Gayatri Plazza, Tata Benz Square, Berhampur - 760 002, (Orissa).**

it can cope with and recover from stresses and shocks and maintain or enhance its capabilities and assets both now and in the future, without undermining the natural resource base. The State of Orissa is situated in the North-Eastern part of the Indian peninsula, with a coast line of 480 km about 8 per cent of the coastline of India. It is bounded by the Bay of Bengal to the east and the States of West Bengal to the North-east, Jharkhand to the North, Chhattisgarh to the West and Andhra Pradesh to the South. There are six maritime districts in the State: Balasore (80 km), Bhadrk (50 km), Jagatsinghpur (67 km), Puri (155 km) and Ganjam (60 km), with Puri district covering more than a third of the coast line (DOF, 1998). According to *Handbook of Fisheries Statistics of Orissa* (2000-01), Orissa has a total of 589 marine and 3289 inland fishing villages. Marine fishery sector at a glance is shown in Table 7.1.

Table 7.1: Marine Fishery Sector in Orissa at a Glance

• % Share of Orissa to the total coast line of India	– 8%
• Marine coastline	– 480 km
• Estimated Marine Fishery potential	– 1,60,900 tonnes
• Present Production	– 1,16,900 tonnes
• Present level of exploitation of the total fishey potential	– 70%
• Continental shelf	– Around 24,000 km^2
• No of Coastal districts	– 10

Coastal Length and Continental Shelf Area in Orissa

Coastal eco-systems have key inbuilt features or functions. The eco-systems involving in primary and secondary production, sustain the flora and fauna, store sediments and organic carbon, essential to the maintenance of food chains. The coastal eco-systems provide foods (fish, oil, gas, minerals) and services (natural defence against storms and tidal waves, recreation and transportation). The coastal eco-systems provide habitat to genetically, ecologically and economically valuable biological organisms (Ramachandran *et al.*, 2000). Thus regions surrounded by favourable coastal length and continental shelf area are having better livelihood options. Districtwise coastal length and continental shelf area in Orissa is shown in Table 7.2. It is revealed from the exhibit that out of the reporting coastal districts, Puri district is having the maximum proportion of coastal length and continental shelf area against the lowest reported in Ganjam district.

Table 7.2: District Wise Coastal Length and Continental Shelf Area of Orissa

Sl No.	Districts	Coastal Length (in Km)	Continental Shelf Area (in Km^2)
1.	Balasore	130 (27.08)	6457 (27.09)
2.	Cuttack	135 (28.12)	6701 (23.24)
3.	Puri	155 (32.29)	7694 (32.28)
4.	Ganjam	60 (12.5)	2978 (12.49)
	All Orissa	480 (100.0)	23830 (100.0)

Marine Fishing Community in Orissa

Historically traditional fish workers of coastal Orissa, except of Balasore district which was part of Bengal Presidency, have been always of Telugu speaking community locally called Nolias. They belong to communities which have been fishing for more than 1000 years, as referred to in literatures of the early Christian era.

In a typical traditional marine fishing household, usually fish catching is done by the male members and the female members are engaged in processing and marketing and other ancillary activities of fishery based households. Net making and repair are the supplementary household activity also performed by the female members. For India as a whole, it has been estimated that women account for 25 per cent of the workforce in fishing and fish farming, for 60 per cent of the workforce in export oriented fish and shellfish processing and 40 per cent of the work force in domestic fish marketing. Altogether, about half a million women are involved in harvest and post harvest operations in the Indian fisheries sector. At the advent of net making machines, the use of machine made nets have reduced the employment of women in net making. Similarly, due to the improved transportation and infrastructure, the production and marketing of dried fish has declined leading to further lack of employment opportunities of fisher women in the fish processing sector, thereby forcing female members of the marine households to other sectors like building and construction activities, agricultural sector as wage earners. The National Workshop on 'Best practices in micro-finance programme for women in coastal fishing communities' indicated that poverty along with widespread absence of rural infrastructure, services such as safe drinking water, electricity, waste and sewage disposal facilities, health care, educational services, all weather link road as well as a lack of adequate housing facilities etc. mostly typify a fishing community in India. With a view to reduce the incidence of poverty among the coastal fishing communities, Micro finance efforts have been directed on the basis of self-help group concept.

Present chapter is an attempt to understand the role of United Artists Association in promoting the livelihood strategy among the marine fishing community in Orissa.

Objectives of the Study

1. To examine the pattern of alternative livelihood opportunities among the marine fishing community and role of all the three tier process of Samudram project in this regard.
2. To study the impact of micro-finance promoted alternative livelihood programme on the income pattern of the member fishing households.

United Artists Association

United Artists Association (UAA), a registered NGO operating at Ganjam in Orissa, in collaboration with action Aid has started UAA-Action Aid Fisherfolf Development Project popularly called Samudram Project since 1993. Under this programme the livelihood diversification programme of the fishing community in four coastal districts of Orissa has been taken up. It is to note that the fishing communities are one of the most backward communities on the ground of lower literacy rate of 8.4 per cent, high infant mortality rate of 159, absence of health and education service infrastructure and lower economic returns from fishing (ICM, 2000). The districts covered under Samudram Project are Ganjam, Puri, Jagatsinghpur, Kendrapara, Bhadrakh and Balasore. Samudram is a federation of fisherwomen SHGs in Orissa. The federation consists of 247 SHGs with 3080 members, who reside in four coastal districts, i.e. Ganjam, Puri, Bhadrak and Balasore. Majority of the SHGs covered under this projest are found in Ganjam (84 SHGs) and Puri (63 SHGs). The federation has a three-tier structure. In villages with a minimum of 2 and a maximum of 18 SHGs, a village level federation called Nari Shakti Sangh (NSS) is formed. This body consists of 7 to 11 members, who elect their office bearers, i.e. president, secretary and treasurer. At the district level, a federation called Zilla Mahila Machimar Sangh (ZMMS) is formed. The function of district level federation is to provide training support and organize sales promotion. Each NSS is represented at the district level federation by three representatives. The main functions of district level federations are to provide training support to SHGs and to assist them in the sale of their products. The NSS also plays a role with regard to health, educational, advocacy and community development matters. Samudram as the state level federation is governed by a board of 18 directors; 15 directors represent the district level federations. The board has three special invitee members, who represent the UAA and the Orissa Traditional Fish Workers Union. As far as micro-finance and credit is concerned the SHGs belonging to Samudram have not been linked with banks for the purpose of obtaining loans in support of the income generating activities carried out by their members. The credit programme, which is operated by Samudram, uses funds provided by an international NGO called Action Aid. INR21, 00000 channeled through UAA have been provided to SHGs for making loans augmented by INR 700,000 from Samudram's own resources. Each SHG pays INR 30 per annum to their NSS. Besides, each member has contributed Rs. 150 to Samudram for becoming its life member. By the end of March 2007, Samudram had a fund of Rs. 7 million, which are used for the purpose of on lending to its members. SHG members are charged an annual rate of interest of 18 per cent on the loans they take. Of the loan interest, SHGs keep 8 per cent towards their administrative expenses while 10 per cent is used for further lending. The coverage of Samudram project is shown in Table 7.3.

Materials and Methods

The socio-economic changes arising out of livelihood diversification programme are explained by analyzing primary data obtained from 20 Fisher Women SHGs promoted under Samudram project in Ganjam District, one of the coastal districts in Orissa. The study also analyses the impact of the intervention on sustainable development of the fishing community on the basis of selected indicators as outlined by Sustainable Development Approach.

Table 7.3: Coverage of Samudram project

Sl. No.	Districts	Blocks	Length of Coastline (km)
1.	Balasore	–	80
2.	Bhadrakh	Basudevpur, Chandabali	50
3.	Kendrapara	Rajnagar, Mahakalpada	68
4.	Jagatsingpur	Balikuda, Ersama	67
5.	Puri	Astarnga, kakatpur, Gop, Krushnaprasad, Puri sadar, Brahmagiri	155
6.	Ganjam	Chhatrapur, Ganjam, Rangeiluna, Chikiti	60
	6 Districts	15 Blocks	480

Source: Arathi Sridhar (2005).

Trend of Marine Fish Production in Ganjam District

Over years the marine fish production in Orissa is found to be almost stagnant. In the year 1985-86, the total marine fish production in Orissa stood at 6.57 thousand tones which showed a declining tendence in the subsequent year's upto 1996-97. In th year 2000-01 it marginally increased 6.78 million tonnes. The reason is attributed to the stagnancy of this sector which is not attracting outsiders' particularly inland fishing community to explore the opportunities in marine fishing.

Financial Needs of the Fishing Community

Despite MFI penetration into rural areas, a large number of informal credit markets still operate widely within these areas. Fishers are one of the most vulnerable targets

Table 7.4: Trend of Marine Fish Production in Ganjam (in 000 tonnes)

Sl. No.	Year	Ganjam	Fish Landing Centres in Ganjam
1.	1985-86	6.57	Gopalpur
2.	1990-91	6.62	Arjipali
3.	1991-92	6.04	Bakshipalli
4.	1992-93	5.66	Nuagoraband
5.	1993-94	6.11	Patisundar
6.	1994-95	5.94	Dighipali
7.	1996-97	6.01	Haripur
8.	2000-01	6.78	Katara
			Sabilla

Source: Statistical Outline of Orissa - 2001.

and often enter into exploitative relationships with money lenders that inhibit them from investing in production, establishing micro-enterprises, or scaling up their activities. One of the most frequently observed money lending schemes is operated by intermediaries. Under this system, fishers borrow money from an intermediary to purchase or repair a boat or to stock up on food and supplies for long fishing voyages. They are then required to sell the catch to the intermediary at 20 to 30 per cent less than the market price instead of selling it directly on the open market. This acts as both principal and interest repayment. Fishers often receive credit from the same intermediaries in case of emergency to cover the expenses of marriage, to repair damaged equipment, or to purchase a new boat. In such situations, borrowers pay interest rates from 60 to 100 per cent per annum. It is common to find fishers who have been unable to break out of the debt cycle and who continue to borrow in order to repay debt. Another practice is one where a boat-less fisherman borrows a boat from a rich person with several boats. The boat owner decides whether to rent the boat out or not after reviewing the expertise and the past record of the fisherman. Under the terms and conditions of acquiring the boat, the fisherman is required to provide a share (65-75%) from the catch to the boat owner. One of the factors accentuating the money lender dependency is that there is often intense competition amongst fishers. Fishers are hunters and gatherers competing for a common yet easily depleted resource. While there are plenty of fish in deep waters, small scale fishermen are unable to reach that distance since the boats they use only allow them to go a limited distance from the shoreline. As a result, people in fishing communities, do not network as much to assist each other in times of need and, in the absence of these safety nets, fishers increasingly turn to moneylenders. Having no access to formal channels of credit or collateral to do so only aggravates this situation. Small scale fishermen, traders and fish processors face the same problem as any other person from poor and marginalized communities: they require small frequent loans and are unable to match collateral requirements of formal financial institutions. Additionally, formal financial institutions do not have the required outreach in terms of branch networks in the areas where small scale fishers live. Apart from business-related loans, there is also a big demand for consumption loans within fishing communities. In short, fishing communities are a good potential target customer segment for MFIs; given that credit products can be developed to service the specific business needs of these communities, there is ample scope for MFIs involvement. Samudram runs five procurement centres for fresh and dry fish, one each at Golabandha, Arjipalli, SanaNolianuagaon, kokherkada, Poddampedarun by trained fisherwomen, churning out products like fish and prawn achar, fisgh papad, fish balls, fish pakoda, fish cutlets, fish cakes and fish paneer.

Training and Marketing

Armed with support from OXFAM, Action Aid, The orissa traditional Fish women's Association (OTFWW) and the college of Fisheries, Rangeilunda, Samudram not only began intensive training programmes for its members but also embarked on a sustainable marketing blitz. With technical assistance from the central institute of Fisheries Education (CIFE), Mumbai, Samudram sells its packaged products in food grade pockets. Table 7.5 points out the value added fish products per SHG during the year 2006-07. Various value added fish products of the SHGs include pickle, Jhuribhujia, Papad and dry papad. It is reported that these products are highly demanded as non-veg snacks items. The mean value of the value added items per SHG is calculated to be Rs. 8,660 for pickle, Rs. 1665 for Jhuri bhujia, Rs. 1220 for *papad* and Rs. 600 for dry *papad.* It is reported that among the salable value-added fishery, fish pickle particularly prawn pickle is largely demanded by the urban customers.

Table 7.5: Value Added Fish Products per SHG in 2006-07

Sl. No.	Value Added Fish Products	Quantity (in kg)	Value (in Rs.)
1.	Pickle	34	8660
2.	Jhuri Bhujia	12	1655
3.	*Papad* (Directly Eatable)	24	1220
4.	Dry *Papad*	20	600

Trading of the Value Added Fish Items

These products are sold through Chennai based companies DSF and RSK; Delhi based King Fisher and Howrah based Starfish, Orient fish, and LF & Co. To explore market potential of value added fish and fish products, two resource agencies 'International Resource for Fairer Trade, Mumbai and XIMB, Bhubaneswar are working for Samudram. Besides these companies, the concerned SHGs also undertake their own sales promotion activities. Out of the different agencies associated with the trading of the value added fishery of Samudram project, Starfish, Howrah and DSF, Chennai are the major marketing partners. In the year 2006-07, DSF, Chennai; and Starfish, Howrah had sales to the extent of Rs. 4,71,223 and Rs. 2,54,506 respectively.

Table 7.6: Fish Transaction of Samudram Members (2006-07)

Sl. No.	Traders	Quantity (in kg)	Sales Amount (in INR)
1.	DSF, Chenneai	4727	471223
2.	Starfish, Howrah	5688	254506
3.	Orient fish, Howrah	276	11070
4.	LF & Co, Howrah	179	7960

Change in the Mean Income of the SHG Households

Due to the support made to SHGs under Samudram project, there have been marginal changes in the mean income of the SHG households. In the year 1995, the mean income was Rs. 15,653 which has increased to Rs. 28,044 in 2009. But this increase in income is certainly not due to the capacity development projects rather due to the dynamics of the market in terms of rising price level of the fish items.

Table 7.7: Trends in the Mean Income among the beneficiary households

Sl. No.	Year	Mean Annual Household Income
1.	1995	15653
2.	2000	22378
3.	2005	24312
4.	2009	28044

Conclusion

The role of United Artists Association in promoting the skills of the marine fishing community is significant. Previously, Fisher Women were ignorant of the value added fishery items. Now-a-days they are slowly adopting the skill, which is leading to a slower increase in their income levels. Full fledged adoption of the learning concequent upon the Samudram's training programme will lead to a better income and consumption patter among the fishing community. It is expected that continuous adoption will lead towards the livelihood sustainability.

REFERENCES

Curran Lynnc, Nancy Natilson and Robbin Young (2006): "Case Study on Profitabilityof Micro Finance in Commercial Banks: Hattan National Bank" in S Rajgopalchari (Ed), *Micro-finance* Case Studies, ICFAI University Press, Hyderabad.

GTZ BRI (1995): "One Hundred Years of Bank Rakyat Indonesia1895-1995", *Jakarta.*

ICM (2002): "Report of the Review Project Activities Conducted during 17-22 June 2002", *Integrated Coastal Management,* Kakinada, Andhra Pradesh.

Muhammad Anu (2009): "Grameen and Micro Credit: A Tale of Corporate Success", *Economic nad Political Weekly,* Vol. XLIV, No. 35.

Panda, R.K (2008): "Socio-Economic Impact of Tribal Self-Help Groups Promoted Under Watershed Programme in Nawarangpur District in Orissa", *ICFAI Journal of Public Administration,* October.

Ramachandran, S., D. Asir Ramesh and V.S. Gowri(2000): "Coastal Ecosystems: Their Problems and Management", *Management of Problems in Coastal Area Ocean Engineering Centre.*

Tietze, U (1985): "*Artisanal Marine Fisherfolk in Orissa: A Techno Demographic Study*", Vidyapuri, Cuttack.

8

Women Entrepreneurship
Issues and Policies

Subhrabala Behera*

Women entrepreneurship needs to be studied separately too two main reasons-the first reason is that women's entrepreneurship has been recognized during the last decade as an important untapped source of economic growth. Women entrepreneurship create new jobs for themselves and others by being different also provide society with different solutions to management, organization and business problems as well as exploitation of entrepreneurial opportunities. However women still represent a minority of all entrepreneurs. Thus there exists a market failure discriminating against women's possibility to become entrepreneurs and their possibility to become successful entrepreneurs. This market failure needs to be addressed by policy makers so that the economic potential of this group can be fully utilized.

The second reason is that topic of 'women in entrepreneurship' has been largely neglected both in society in general and the social sciences (Brush & Hisrich, 1999; Holmquist & Sundin, 2002). Not only have women lower

---

* **Ph.D., Political Science, Utkal University, BBSR.**

participant in entrepreneurship than men but they also generally choose to start and manage firms in different industries than men tend to be. The industries (primarily retail, education and other service industries) choosen by women are often or have until recently been perceived as being less important to economic development and growth than high technology and manufacturing. Furthermore mainstream research, policies and programmes tend to be "men streamed" too often do not take into account the specific needs of women entrepreneurs and would be women entrepreneurs. As a consequence, equal opportunity between men and women from the perspective of entrepreneurship is not a reality. To facilitate progress, more work needs to be done in order to:

- Better understand the function of women's entrepreneurship in society and for economic development:- We know that women entrepreneurship play a non-trivial role in the economy that they face challenges and obstacles different from those faced by men and that they will act differently. The larger the difference is between men and women entrepreneurship and the more different we can expect their relative contribution to economic development to be.
- Better understand the impact of women's entrepreneurship in different economic contexts:-By contexts we mean both the economic and the societal level of development when it comes to the role of women in society. For example, we know that women's entrepreneurship in transition and developing countries is quantitatively different from developed countries. For example, the problems of Eastern Europe are different because these economics have gone through and still undergoing changes to adapt to a market economy. In these countries women and men were under the communist regime, supposedly equal in all respect of society. In developing countries

combination of poverty, low levels of formal education and women having a very low social status creates special challenges for women engaging in entrepreneurship. In developed countries women have access to the same education and jobs as men but important difference still exist and they seem to be shrinking at a very slow space.

Obstacles

There are two types of obstacles in the way of women entrepreneurship:

1. **General obstacles:** women engaging in entrepreneurship (opportunity recognition and willingness to start firms).
2. **Specific obstacles:** start-ups [assembling necessary information, financial and human resources to start a firm], specific obstacles to managing a small firm and growing firms.

General Obstacles

1. *The lack of role models in entrepreneurship.*

   There exists a strong connection between the presence of role models and the emergence of entrepreneurs (Shapero and Sokol, 1982) and women as they historically have not been present as entrepreneurs in general lack close role models.

2. *Lack of experience*

   All stages in entrepreneurship are depended on relevant experience, from the identification of opportunities to the execution of running a business. Human capital theory posits that individuals with or higher quality human capital achieve higher performance in executing relevant task (Becker, 1975). Depending on their levels of human capital individuals differ in their ability to discover and exploit opportunities, which depends largely on previous education and work experience. But because of both demand and supply factors women lack the experience needed to identify and exploit opportunities.

3. *Lack of relevant networks and of societal position*

   Women have in general a lower social position than men, which affects the kind of network they can access or are part of entrepreneurship. Women have therefore less access to critical resources, support and information needed to successfully start and manage a new firm compared to men.

4. *Lack of wealth*

   A prerequisite for starting a firm is to have capital in terms of financial assets and knowledge assets. Women's position in society has led to a lack of assets in both these aspects. The constraints of family obligations make it harder for women to take on work on a full-time basis and to engage in a career. This in turn decreases the range of possible work opportunities for women leading to jobs in lower paid sectors, which is not a good basis for creating personal wealth.

Specific Obstacles

Obstacles specific to starting a new firms.

External Finance and Sex Discrimination

In general women have lower personal financial assets than men. This means that for a given opportunity and equally capable individual women must secure additional resources compared to men in order to exploit the opportunity because they control less capital.

Obstacles Specific to Managing a Small Firm

It is emphasized that women and men have different access to entrepreneual opportunities. These differences can be explained in terms of in the fundamental discrepancy in the primary roles of women and men and of the profound impact of the gendered work structure. It is reviewed the factors explaining this in terms of *inter alia*, educational and industrial segregation. However, what happens to the women that overcome these barriers when it comes to education, experience, wealth, and who are actually managing a firm?

Obstacles Specific to Growing Firms

A specific problem of women entrepreneurs seems to be their in ability to achieve growth especially sales growth (Du Rictz and Henrekson, 2000). As discussed previously, lack of motivation might to be a contributing factor. Basically women because of having greater day-to-day responsibility to the family have less time to invest in the development of their firms.

Key Policy Recommendations

Based on these findings, policy measures to support women's entrepreneurs can go alone some different lines. Policy makers can:

- **Increase the ability of women:** To participate in the labour force by ensuring the availability affordable child care and equal treatment in the work place. More generally, improving the position of women in society and promoting entrepreneurship generally will have benefits in terms of women's entrepreneurship.
- **Listen to the voice of women entrepreneurship:** The creation of government offices which could have program responsibility such as providing women's business centre organizing business seminars and meetings and providing web-based information to women who are already entrepreneurs and who have important insights into the changes needed to improve women entrepreneurs.

- **Incorporate a women entrepreneurial dimension in the formation of all SME-related policies:** This can be done by ensuring that the impact on women's entrepreneurship is taken at the design stage.
- **Promote the development of women entrepreneurship network:** These are major sources of knowledge about women's entrepreneurship and valuable tools for its development and promotion. Cooperation and partnerships between national and international networks can facilitate entrepreneurial endeavors by women in a global economy.
- **Periodically evaluate the impact of only SME-related to policies** on the success of women-owned businesses and the extent to which such businesses take advantage of them. The objective should be to identify the ways to improve the effectiveness of those that should be retained. Good practices that are identified in this way should be disseminated and shared internationally.
- **Improve the factual and analytical underpinnignes of our understanding of the role of women entrepreneurship in the economy**. This requires strengthening the statistical basis for carrying out gender-equality cross-country comparative analyses and longitudinal studies of the impact of important developments and policies especially over time.

Conclusion

From an Australian economic prospective we have analyzed the characteristics of women's entrepreneurship and offered a set of policy recommendations. As we still do not know enough of the entrepreneurial process and women we have argued that better knowledge about the economic importance of women's entrepreneurship and their particular strengths, weakness and opportunities, is central. As low rates of women's entrepreneurship are both related to status of women and the status of entrepreneurship. We have suggested that increasing the abilities of women to participate in the labour force and generally to improve the position of women in society and generally increase the possibility to engage in entrepreneurship in central. However, more targeted initiatives are also needed to support women entrepreneurs and would be entrepreneurs.

REFERENCES

Brush, C., and Hisrich, R.D. 1999,Women-owned Businesses: Why do they Matter? In: Z.J. Acs (Ed.) *Are Small Firms Important? Their Role and Impact: III-127*, Boston, M.A.: Kluwer Academic Publisher.

Carter, S. Anderson, S., and Shaw, E. 2001,*Women's Business Ownership: A Review of the Academic, Popular and Internet Literature*, London, UK, Small Business Service.

Gatewood, E.J. Carter, N.M., Brush, C.G., Greene, P.G., and Hart, M.M. (Eds.) 2003. *Women Entrepreneurship, Their Ventures and the Venture Capital Industry: An Annotated Bibliography*, Stockholm: E & BRI.

The Prime Minister's Task Force on Women Entrepreneurship: Report and Recommendations, 2003, Canada and www.liberal. Parl.gc.ca/entrepreneur.

9

Challenges of Self-help Groups for Poverty Alleviation and Women Empowerment

S.S. Nayak*
V. Siba Prakash**

Introduction

The Country has witnessed a rapid growth of self-help groups (SHGs) in the last one decade or so. The SHG growth which has almost assumed the form of a movement represents a massive grassroots level mobilisation of poor rural women into small informal associations capable of forging links with formal systems to help access financial and other services needed for their socio-economic advancement. Basically, SHGs are being promoted as a part of the microfinance interventions aimed at helping the poor to obtain easily financial services like savings, credit and insurance.

The promotion of SHGs in India began more formally in 1992 with the launch of the SHG-Bank Linkage

* Senior Faculty, Department of Commerce, R.N. College, Dura, Berhampur, (Orissa).

** Ph.D., Scholar, M.B.A., Deptt. Berhampur University, Berhampur, (Orissa).

Programme by National Bank for Agricultural and Rural Development (NABARD). The programme's main aim was to improve rural poor's access to formal credit system in a cost effective and sustainable manner by making use of SHGs.

A self-help group has been defined as a small and informal association of poor having preferably similar socio-economic background and who have come together to realise some common goals based on the principles of self-help and collective responsibility. SHGs become relevant because of the following reasons. First, a SHG working on the principle of solidarity helps the poor to come together to pool their savings and access credit facilities. A SHG by tapping social capital like trust and reciprocation helps in replacing physical collateral, a major hurdle faced by the poor in obtaining formal credit. Then, through the principles of joint liability and peer pressure, a SHG ensures prompt loan recovery from the members. In the process, a SHG helps the poor, especially women, to establish their credit-worthiness.

The second major role of SHGs is seen in terms of their potential to empower the women members. The participation in SHG and the access obtained to savings and credit can play a transformational role for women, socially and economically. The access to savings and credit helps a women member to take care of her family's financial needs for consumption and production purposes. The ability to meet such needs of the family would enhance the standing of the woman in the family leading to better gender relations. The continued participation in SHG is further likely to enhance the awareness, skills and other abilities of the women resulting in building of individual self-esteem and in getting due social recognition.

The SHG programme is now more than a decade old. There is a need to explore:

1. to what extent SHGs have helped poor women to get access to savings and credit?
2. to what extent the improved access to financial capital has contributed towards attaining goals like poverty alleviation and women's empowerment? and
3. what are the challenges and constraints faced by SHGs in playing their expected role?

The primary role expected of SHGs is one of improving for the poor the access to savings and credit. Studies available indicate that as a result of the participation in SHGs, members have been able to accumulate significant savings. In States such as Andhra Pradesh, on an average, SHG members have accumulated individual savings worth up to Rs. 1,800. In mature SHGs the average individual savings has been as high as Rs. 10,000. Though in absolute amount the savings is small, it becomes significant when seen from the angle that bulk of the SHG members hail from poorer communities unable to save conveniently and safely earlier. Own savings can be handy and useful in many ways. Many SHGs members even consider development of the habit of savings as the major impact of their participation in SHGs. There are evidence to indicate that using the opportunity of savings provided by the SHGs, women are able to meet various life cycle needs like housing, education and marriage.

The SHGs are also found helping women to leverage the savings for accessing credit. SHGs are utilising the savings mobilised to lend small loans internally among their members. A significant number of SHGs have now taken up internal lending helpful for meeting urgent consumption and social credit needs. Based on the savings accumulated, SHGs are borrowing from banks and SHG federations to meet bigger credit needs of the members for production purposes. More and more SHGs are getting credit linked to banks which is increasing the members' access to formal sources of credit.

Impact on Poverty

A foremost impact discernible is the reduced dependence of SHG households on informal sources of credit. The members of the SHGs have been able to reduce their dependence on moneylender very significantly. A study on SHGs reported a decline in the share of moneylender's loan from 66 to 15 per cent for the members. In another study, nearly 51 per cent of the members closed their old debt with the moneylenders using SHG loans. The members at the same time have been able to generate a substantial surplus for themselves due to cheaper interest paid on loans.

Through credit obtained from SHGs, the members have made efforts both to protect their families from various vulnerabilities as well as build their economic base to escape from poverty. This is evident from the fact that members are making use of SHG loans for diverse purposes. While use of loan for consumption purpose still remains a major item of utilisation, members are increasingly using the SHG loans for social and productive needs. Health education and housing are some of the areas members have begun to increasingly channelise their loans. In Tamil Nadu, it was found that nearly 14 per cent loan had been used for housing purpose. In Andhra Pradesh it was found that nearly 6 per cent of the members had utilized their loan for children's education.

The SHG members are also using quite significantly SHG loans for regular economic activities like animal husbandry, agriculture and petty business. This is evident from the fact that nearly 74 per cent of SHG members in Tamil Nadu have invested in creating various assets like land, livestock, and household durables after joining SHGs.

On the contrary, there are also studies which have found only a limited impact of SHGs. A study concluded that microfinance seems to have played a more critical role in facilitating clients to cope with situations rather than deal with life cycle events in a sustainable manner. The economic impact of SHGs has been more protectional rather than promotional in nature. This is attributed to exclusion of very poor and the general constraints faced by poor in making use of loan for productive investments. There are also some evidence to suggest that the participation in SHG has even led to change for worse on many counts.

Though SHGs have begun to contribute in improving the economic conditions of the poor households, the impact does not seem to be a uniform phenomenon. At the same time, there is no evidence to establish the fact that the positive impact noticed in some instances are attributable to women's involvement. However, going by the evidence available from Bangladesh, it could be inferred that the involvement of women might have made a significant difference even in India wherever positive changes have been noticed.

Women's Empowerment

Given the widespread gender bias against women in various fields, there are arguments that interventions like microfinance have the potential to enhance women's capabilities which can make a significant difference to overall development of women. Those who hold the above view argue for supporting microfinance interventions and tuning them to meet the needs of women specifically. On the other hand, there are arguments that microfinance interventions can at best have only a very limited impact in empowering women. Interventions like microfinance are constrained by the existing socio-cultural structures like patriarchy in order for them to make a very a significant impact on women. Under such circumstances women hardly have any control in deciding or directing loan use for purposes, which can enhance their individual economic position over those dictated by familial requirements. Access to savings and credit can take care of mainly the practical needs of women instead of meeting their strategic needs.

A study which looked at the changes brought about by longer association of members with their SHGs concluded that: members of the old SHGs emerged as more confident, financially more secure, more in control of their lives, and in a stronger position *vis-a-vis* their family members. The personal abilities, ownership of economic assets, development of skills, ability to decide about self and extent of participation in political sphere are likely to improve for the better if the women members continue to participate in SHGs for a longer period.

At the same time, there evidence which tell us that microfinance and SHGs may not always lead to transformational impact on women. A study found that women have certainly become more visible as microfinance clients, but being a clients does not translate automatically into empowerment. The study found only mixed evidence about the role of microfinance in either increasing women's economic activity or increasing women's awareness, mobility and skill development or enhance women's status in the household as income contributors and decision makers . The study, however observed that between different models of micro-finance, the SHG model seems to show better scope for developing women's opportunities and skills.

Challenges

What are the constraints and challenges facing the SHG programme to contribute more effectively for poverty alleviation and empowerment?

A Problem of SHG Outreach

The SHG programmes show a very skewed growth pattern in the country. The programme is largely concentrated in southern region of the country. It is important that the micro-finance programmes spread more evenly so that the benefits are available especially in regions where the need is more accurate. This calls for increased investment in SHG formation and development by banks and government. The programmes have to orient themselves to the needs of the very poor as the existing SHG models have not been able to cover this section significantly.

Restrictive Policies of Formal Agencies

The second major constraint faced by SHGs is the continued restrictive loan policies of the commercial banks. The commercial banks took a long time to clearly recognise and internalise the concept. The SHG model is primarily a savings based model. The commercial banks have been following largely 1: 4 savings-credit ratio prescribed more as a norm for lending. Even the loan terms are uniformly prescribed. The SHGs having lower savings ability find the lending ratio highly restrictive. As a result, many SHGs are unable to access credit adequately. This is forcing SHG members to restrict loan size/period and even distribute loan amount equally. There are instances of SHG members going back to moneylenders. In many cases banks are also not able to give adequate time to SHGs forcing SHGs to operate more in ways which suit banks than the SHGs. If SHGs, whose strengths lies in informality, have to make a better impact, the formal system has to tune itself to the needs of SHGs and their members. This calls for adopting highly proactive and innovative policies to deal with the SHGs.

SHG Quality and Leadership

The performance of SHGs to a great extent depends upon their quality of governance and management. Available evidence clearly suggests that the quality of SHGs has suffered due to their fast growth. In Andhra Pradesh which is one of the leading states in SHG formation, it was found that about one-third of SHGs were of unsatisfactory quality with regard to their organisational and financial management abilities. It is also found that as SHGs grow older their quality further deteriorates. In many cases SHGs even break down or wind-up their operations. The major reasons attributed for the poor quality of SHGs are: target based promotion of SHGs, inadequate training and capacity building, and widespread illiteracy of the members. Continued and specialized trainings can help develop the abilities of SHGs in maturing fully.

Another area of concern is SHG leadership. SHGs have nurtured some exceptional leaders who have excelled both in managing their SHGs and contributing to the sphere of village development. But it is also found that SHG leaders have benefited relatively more from their SHGs both financially and in terms of development of individual abilities as compared to other members. It is necessary that SHGs benefit other members in a similar way. The promoting agencies need to help in broadbasing the leadership of SHGs.

Development of Skills and Linkages

The success of SHGs in contributing to poverty alleviation and empowerment depends on the ability of members to take up newer and productive investment activities. Even where there is positive impact, it has been found that SHG members have utilised the loans mainly in conventional activities like agriculture, animal husbandry and petty business. Such an investment pattern has resulted mainly in women channelising their loans to meet mainly the needs of other household members.

This calls for separate policy interventions wherein efforts are made to develop the entrepreneurial skills of women and linkage to obtain technology, raw materials and marketing channels. Policies are required to reserve or show preference in allotting various schemes like PDS, mid-day meal and IT – enabled services to SHGs. Training and exposure to SHG members on interventions managed by women should also become an essential part of the SHG development.

Conclusion

There is a massive mobilization of women taking place as a result of the SHG movement. The growth of SHGs incidentally has occurred during the economic reforms' period. The SHG movement has a good potential to serve both as a human face of the economic reforms as well as contribute towards women's emancipation. There is a major onus on all actors involved in SHG promotion and development to further intensify their efforts in enabling SHGs to reach a mature stage. We need a major investment in capacity building of SHGs and proactive policies to help overcome the constraints faced by SHGs to integrate them fully into the developmental programmes aimed at women's empowerment.

REFERENCES

Das, Biswaroop (2005) *Micro-finance and Rural Credit Markets: A Study of Clients Using Micro-Credit in Gujarat and Maharashtra*, Ahmedabad: Friends of Women's World Banking.

DHAN Foundation (2004) *The Impact of Kalanjiam Community Banking Programme*, Madurai: Dhan Foundation.

MYRADA (2002) “Impact of Self-help Groups on the Social Empowerment Status of Women Members in Southern India”, *Paper Presented at the Seminar on SHG-Bank Linkage Programme* at New Delhi on 25-26, November 2002.

Puhazhendhi, V. and Badatya (2002) *Self-help Group Bank Linkage Programme for Rural Poor in India: An Impact Assessment*, Mumbai: NABARD.

Reddy, Raja (2005) A Study on Self-help Group (SHG) - Bank Linkage in Andhra Pradesh. Hyderabad: APMAS.

Sinha, Frances, *et.al.* (2005) "Micro-finance and Gender Development: Assessing the Impact" in: *Gender and Micro-finance*, Ahmedabad: Friends of Women's World Banking.

Women Entrepreneurship in India

Dr. Bandana Gaur*
R.L. Panigrahy**

Introduction

Being women constitute half of the total population, still they are the largest group who are deprived off major benefits of development. In India, the work participation rate of women is less than half that of the men. There is continuing concentration of women is low paid and low occupation status which indicate that women are marginalized in the labour force. There is a common assumption that man are the bread winners and that most of the female work is either done in the leisure time or serves as the procurer of supporting income for the family.

Empowerment is the process to delegate power or authority to, or to give ability to, or enable or permit the target. In fact, 'Empowerment' is a multi-dimensional process which should enable individuals to relies there full identity and powers in all spheres of life. It consists of greater access

* **Faculty (Sociology), EDI, Agra.**

** **Faculty (Management), ACMT, Berhampur (Orissa).**

to knowledge and resources greater autonomy in decision-making to enable them to have greater ability to plan their lives, or have greater control over the circumstances that influence their lives and free them from shackles imposed on them by custom, belief and practice. In general, development with justice is exposed to generate the forces that lead to employment of various section of population in a country and to uplift their living standard.

Entrepreneurship can help women's economic independence and improve their social status. Automatically the women get empowered once they attain economic independence. The development of women entrepreneurship enables society to understand and appreciate their abilities. It enhances their status and leads to integration of women in nation-building and economic development. It provides the needed psychological satisfaction and imbibes a deep sense of achievement to create their enhanced identity in society.

Women Entrepreneurship in India

Pandit Jawaharlal Nehru, the first Prime Ministry of India observed:

> "freedom depends on economic conditions even more than political. If a women is not economically free and self-earning, she will have to depend on her husband or some one else and dependents are never free."

As a result of this, a new perspective came into existence. Women were encouraged to get higher education at par with man. Facilities were provided for women to get new jobs and enter into every walk of life. Gradually, the phenomenon of women entrepreneurship entered into development economics. Celebration of International Women's Year in 1975 has marked a significant improvement in women's development and however research on women is of recent phenomenon. The Industrial

Policy Resolution of 1991 had highlighted the necessity to provide special training programmes to develop women entrepreneurship.

In the Sixth Five-Year Plan women are encouraged for self-employment. It provided a package of services to women entrepreneurs who wanted to launch self-employment. On 30 December 1987 in Bombay a new organization called, All India Manufactures, Organization (AIMO) was set up with a view to encourage, motivate and provide guidance to prospective women entrepreneurs to set up industries. It also aimed to disseminate information connected with policies and schemes available and not only equal rights and privileges for women but also making special provision for women. By the 73rd and 74th Constitutional Amendments, one-third of seats in the local bodies of panchayat and municipalities have been allotted to women and thus laying a strong foundation for their participation in decision-making process at the village and district levels. There is also greater awareness among Indian women about entrepreneurship as a career. The growing awareness is mainly due to the fact that the profile of Indian women has undergone perceptible change during the recent past. It is well documented fact that number of women in the universities and technical institution are growing. There is evidence of a direct relationship between their growth of women's education and their number in all the functional areas. The pessimistic view of society towards women is being replaced by modern outlook.

Contribution of Women Entrepreneurship Towards Social Development

1. **Contribution in Economic Development:** The contribution of the women in the field of economic development is very important for the participation of the women in industries has improved not only economic condition of their family but also help in economic progress of the country.

2. **Problem of Unemployment:** In India there is a problem of unemployment which in the main of poverty. Women entrepreneurship has played an important role in eradication of problem of unemployment. Several women entrepreneurs have established industrial unit which has provided employment to unemployment persons. This has reduced the problem of employment some extent.

3. **Eradication of the Social Evils:** There are many social evils persisting in the society due to women entrepreneurship. Various social evils like, child marriage prohibited widow marriage, dowry system, female feticide, illiteracy among the girl child are showing declining trend. On observing the status of women entrepreneurship their women also accepting various trades, by ignoring old customs, rituals restrictions on them. Now women has come out of their homes and joined various services, business, leadership etc. This has itself the eradication of veil system (*parda* system).

4. **Self-dependence:** Traditionally women are dependent for their money matters and family decisions, on men. But due to entrance of women entrepreneurs in the industrial sector they have achieved self dependence. It had increased their social stratus and self-confidence and. Now they are not subordinate of men but they play role of colleagues.

5. **Development of Leadership:** Women entrepreneurship creates a quality of leadership and women takes lead in different areas. It benefits in social development of society and rearing of children in family.

Difficulties in the Development of Women Entrepreneurship

Women entrepreneurs encounter many problems in India. Very few women entrepreneurs are in big enterprises.

They are mostly confined to small scale industries. They face lot of problems in establishing and running of business and running of business and most of the problems are connected to finance and management.

1. **Social attitude:** this is regarded as the most important stumbling black in the path of women entrepreneurship. Despite constitutional equality, there is wider spread discrimination against women. In a male dominated society women do not get equal treatment. This is specially so in the rural area of India. Rural women have the potential, but they lack adequate training. There is common belief that skill imparted to a girl is lost when she gets married. Therefore, girls continue to be helpers in agriculture and handicrafts and the rigid attitude prevent them from becoming successful and dependent entrepreneurs.
2. **Lack of Education:** In India around 3/5th or 60% of women are still illiterate. Illiteracy is the root cause of social economics problems. Due to the lack of education and that too qualitative education, women are not aware of business, technology and market knowledge. Also lack of education cause low achievement motivation among women. This lack of education creates lot of problems in the setting up and running of business enterprises.
3. **Low Mobility:** Unlike men women mobility in India is limited. She is not in position to travel frequently and be away for longer periods. Thus, her mobility is restricted. This also has an implication on business.
4. **Families Ties Up:** in India it is mainly a women's duty to look after the children and other members of the family. Support and approval of husbands seen necessary condition for women entry into the business.
5. **Intense Competition:** women entrepreneurs do not have organization set up is a lot of money for

canvassing and advertisement. Thus they have to face a stiff competition for marketing their product with both their male counterparts such a competition ultimately results in the liquidation of women enterprises.

6. **Problem of Finance:** Women entrepreneurs suffer from shortage of finance as they do not generally have property on their names to use them as collateral for obtaining funds from external sources.

7. **Gender Difference:** Gender has always been an important factor discussed for entrepreneurial activity like all entrepreneurs, suffer from inadequate financial resources and working capital. The lead access to external funds due to their inability to provide tangible security Bank have also taken a negative attitude while providing finance. For women entrepreneurs. The result in women entrepreneurs are forced to rely on their own savings and loans from family friends. The quantum of such funds is often negligible leading to failure of enterprise.

Strategy of Development of Women Entrepreneurship

- To motivate women to come out of their traditional perception and responsibilities some psychological and social changes have to be inculcated in the system.
- Women have the need to put more efforts to change people attitude, to aspire women in the society at large:
  - Women have to be stimulated to take right kind of action at right time.
- Successful women in the field of entrepreneurship have to help other women in starting and sustaining in their business whole-heartedly.
- All women entrepreneurs should join together and from co-operative societies to see their industries run effectively.

- Promotion of women entrepreneurship as an important and valued component has to be taken care of.
- Women entrepreneurship research and application from time to time have to be documented.
- The government policy makers to re-evaluate the strategies on women education and their entrepreneurial development and it should be planned and implemented.
- Women should be made aware of various credit facilities, financial incentives and subsidies.
- To see women entrepreneurs' development sustainable, a constant re-enforcement is required.
- Thought it is necessary to help them, to initiate their enterprise, a constant follow- up and liberal financial support should be ensured to enable them in functioning and smooth running of their enterprise.

Suggestion for the Development of Women Entrepreneurship

Thus we can say that women face lots of problems in the male dominated society. There are many unwritten rules, which the society scrupulously follows. Most of the rules pertain to women and encompass a wide variety of social activity like women's education, their employment hours of work, dress outing, and the like can interact only with known persons.

The following suggestions are made to solve the problems of women entrepreneurs:

- Control and state government should assist women entrepreneurs to participate in international trade fair, exhibition and conferences.
- Several policy initiatives have been made by the government like Manila smoky, Swarnajayanthi, Gram Swarojgar yojna (SGSY), Development of Women and

Children of Rural Areas (DWCRA), Indira Awas Yojana (IAY) and many other policies. Recently the government has enacted the National Policy for the Empowerment of Women, 2001. The goal of the policy is to bring about the advancement development and empowerment of women.

- The family members of women enterpreners should also activity participate and extended all possible support in the matter of managing units set up at by women enterprenetrs.
- Efforts should be made in the direction of simplification of the procedures. Formalities, rules and regulations, etc. required to be fulfilled by the women entrepreneurs in all matter of registration of their and seeking assistance, subsidies, concessions, relief etc, from different departments and governments sponsored organization involved in providing a variety of services to women entrepreneurs.
- Every educated women can take it up as a moral responsibility to support the women entrepreneur come across in their daily lines, either in the boutiques, beauty parlor, or at the fast food ceritens, etc, in any manners to her. The support could be if not a motivational guidance, information related to the business, some counseling etc, women entrepreneurs can set up association whose main objective could be to support and help budding women entrepreneurs.

Conclusion

In present context, modernisation, urbanisation, globalization and development of education, with increasing awareness, women are now seeking gainful participation in several fields. The entrepreneurship among women will help them in earning money and becoming economically independent. Due to social networking women will develop self-confidence, awareness and ability to marshall environmental support. This will lead to an improvement is not only the women, from the point of view of better health, education and skill but an improvement in her living condition also by being able to use cleaner fuel, better house, better sanitation, facilities and infrastructural facilities. This will lead to saving of resources like time, energy, transforming women into stronger personality and an overall improvement in her quality of life.

REFERENCES

Akhauri, M.M.P and S.P. Mishra, "Enterpreneurship Education, A Concept of Approach and Methodology", *Indian Management*, 29 (11-12), November-December, 1990.

Bose, A. "Information Technology and Women Entereneurs", *Third Concept*, April 2006. p. 45.

Business Today, "The 25 Most Powerful Women in Indian Business" September 26, 2004.

Gupta, C.B and Shrinivasan, N.P.(2005), *Entrepreneurship Development in India*, Sultan Chand and Sons, New Delhi.

Loganathan, Siva, K, "Women Enterpreneurs: Problem and Prospects", *Indian Economic Panorma*. Vol. 12, No. 2, July 2002.

Raheem, A. Abdul and C. Prabhu "*Women Entrepreneurs: Problems and Prospects. India: Economic Empowerment of Women*. New Century Publications, New Delhi, India, 2007.

Ramya, N. "Problems of Women Enterpreneurs" *Third Concept* August 2006. p. 39.

Saritha, R. "Women Enterpreneurship: Problem and Need For Environmental Alterations India" *Economic Empowerment of Women* P.M. 57, 2007.

Sharma, Anjuli, Vandana Kaushik, Indian Rural Women and Entrepreneueship. *Third Concept,* November 2007, P.N. 51.

Sugura, B., "Planning for Economic Empowerment of Women" *Social Welfare*, 2001.

11

Market Synergy Between SHGs and Organised Retail Malls in Ganjam District

A Paradigm Towards Leadership Among SHGs

Dr. Radha Krushna Panda*

Introduction

Ganjam district is one of the coastal districts in Orissa. Like other coastal districts, its economy is predominantly agrarian. More than 60 per cent of the total population resides in rural areas and agriculture is their chief occupation. Among the rural households poverty is reported in different clusters and social groups. Secondary data indicate that the SC, ST, landless agricultural labourers of the district are the victims of poverty. To tackle the problems of poverty along with multiple anti-poverty programmes, micro-finance programme through Self-help Groups has been launched in the district since early 1990s, which is found to be continuing at an accelerated pace. The District Administration of Ganjam district, Mission Shakti, a nodal

* **Faculty in Economics and Quantitative Methods, Indian Institute of Professional Studies (IIPS), Gayatri Plazza, Tata Benz Square, Berhampur - 760 002, (Orissa).**

micro-finance promoting agency in Orissa and NABARD are providing wholesome facilitation for the promotion and expansion of the programme. But one thing is found to be lacking i.e. their sustainability aspects which are attributed to improper product development, and improper market development. Interventionists are interested for the sustainability of micro-finance programme towards permanent termination of poverty and improvement of the socio economic fabric of rural households. On the other hand, the prime urban centre Berhampur in the district has been able to attract many organized retailers to the district. At present Vishal Mega Mart, The World and Kolkata Bazar are the important retail malls working in the district. Most of the products sold through these malls and products produced and sold by the SHGs are common. In this backdrop, we propose that if the malls purchase these common products from the SHGs and sell them through their shelves; it can be profitable proposition to both of them and it would be more favourable to SHGs through multi level-value additions and possibly they could emerge as the business leaders.

Need of this Business Plan

It is observed that some of the products which are sold through malls are originated in SME sector, which could also be produced through cottage industries. For examples the products such as pickles, *papads*, jam and jelley, spice powders, spice pastes, processed *dals* and rice, puffed rice, foot mats, readymade garments, paintings, wall hangings etc. are sold by both the parties under study. But with respect to production, the organized retailers depend on others for the finished products. On the other hand SHGs are producers as well as sellers. In this respect retailers can depend on SHGs for the mentioned common items. In this process, SHGs need not bother about the marketing of their products. On the other hand it would also be cheaper on the part of the retailers to procure the finished items to maintain their merchandise. By little value addition in terms of labelling, maintaining consistent quality would make the SHGs viable. On the other hand, some of the other products sold by the retailers could also be sold through SHGs. Thus, organized retailers would find an easy entry to the rural area and SHGs would find a better marketing access to the urban area. Thus simultaneous growth of the urban as well as rural market could establish better consumer base and broad based market. As both the parties would gain, thus proposed business plan is a Win-Win Strategy. Perhaps this is the social desirability of the proposed project.

Objectives

- Ensuring sustainability of the micro-finance programme in Ganjam District.
- Promoting Synergy between self-help groups and retail malls operating in Ganjam district.
- Widening the scope of the market for both of them.
- Promotion of ethno-cultural products in the market.
- Socio-economic betterment in the rural areas.

Consumer Segment

It is to be noted that due to synergy between SHGs (Party-1) and Retails Malls (Party-2) in Ganjam District, there will be a broad consumer segment, especially because party-1's products would be sold in urban areas. Similarly some of the products sold by party-2 could also be targeted to rural consumers through the network of existing SHGs in all parts of the ganjam district.

Targeting the Consumer Segment

The district is fast developing in the micro-credit through SHGs. These SHGs in the district are promoted through Block-level Mahila Sanchayika Sangha (B'MASS) of district Administration, various NGOs working in the District, Mission Shakti Programme of the State Government of Orissa, VVV clubs promoted by NABARD. At present, there are 15529 SHGs comprising 1,90,000 members with a total credit flow of Rs. 34.7 crores covering all the 22 blocks. Ganjam district has the unique distinction of forming federation of women SHGs at block and district levels. Besides there is an increasing trend in credit flow to rural non-farm sector as the district is covered under District Rural Industries Project (DRIP). The members of the SHGs have been pursuing a number of economic activities. The activities pursued by the SGHs members are summarized below in Table 11.1.

Table 11.1: Economic Activities Pursued by the members of the SHGs in Ganjam District

Sl. No	Micro-economic Actiovities	% of SHG Members
1	2	3
1.	*Papad* Making	6
2.	Pickle Making	4
3.	Sweets and confectionary	3
4.	Snacks	4
5.	Processed Rice, puffed Rice, Press Rice	8
6.	Breakfast Cereals	7
7.	Handloom Works	6
8.	Dry Fish and Fish Snacks	3
9.	Carpet making	2
10.	Foot Mates	1
11.	*Pata Chitra* and Other wall hangings	1
12.	Sea Shell Works	1
13.	*Dhkra* Casting and Bell Metal Works	2

(Contd...)

1	2	3
14.	Wood Carving	1
15.	*Agarbatti* and candle making	5
16.	Phenyl making	1
17.	Tomato Ketchup and other Sauces	3
18.	Readymade garments and tailoring	2
19.	Seasons" Greetings	4
20.	Others	36
	Total	**100**

An official visit of our team to the organized retail malls operating in Berhampur city observed that all of the above items shown in Table 11.1 are sold through their outlets. In this background, it is possible to sell those items through the outlets of the organized retailers. Further interviews with the functionaries of those retail outlets suggest that the organized retailers are also interested to enter into the rural markets. But due to certain risks, they are not able to open their outlets in the semi-urban and rural areas. As the network of SHGs is found in the knock and corner of the rural area of Ganjam district, through them it is possible to sell some of their items. Thus, urban customers are the target market of the SHG products and rural market is the target market of Retail malls.

Product Positioning

As per NCAER's estimates, for the first time in India's history, the proportionate share of high middle income group has surpassed to that of the low income group. Further studies also indicate that now-a-days rural customers are much oriented towards life style products and branded products. On the other hand urban customers are interest for the ethno-cultural type of products as produced by the SHGs. Thus various type of life style products marketed by the retail malls would be positioned to rural customers through SHG members. Due to the enormous presence of SHGs in the rural areas and as exclusively women are the members of the SHGs, thus SHGs could be able to influence ruaral consumption decisions. Similarly SHG products with suitable labelling and consistent quality could be positioned to the urban customers.

Value Proposition

- Socio-cultural factors drive a major part of the consumers' psychology. Consume's always and everywhere look at the cultural aspects while purchasing the products. When they know that the product is locally manufactured by the SHGs, there will be better demand for the products. One example may we site that the packaged pickles such as Priya, Dukes and Nilam are not the preferred brands among Berhampur people, instead they prefer local pickle. The major reason being that the consumers are not sure about the ingredients of the packaged pickles. Thus the socio-cultural gaps could be fulfilled through our proposed project.
- SHG products could be substituted for the similar products sold and marketed by the retailers.
- Branding, labelling and consistent quality could drive continuous demand for the SHGs' products. Thus, due to better market access, it would be economically beneficial for the rural SHG members.
- In the long-run, the benefits out of market synergy could lead to overall development in the rural household level.
- Similarly retailers could be able to sell different products particularly life style products in the rural areas.
- Due to synergy, there could be value addition for both the parties under discussion.

Launch and Market Entry Plan

As per our business plan, liasioning could be initiated by the SHG promoting agencies operating at the district level, State level and national level. They can direct to the malls to consider SHG products for selling on priority basis. The licensing to the organized retailers should be linked with capacity building at the SHG level. On the other hand Retailers Association of India should come forward to implement the programme towards a win-win possibility. For a vibrant business environment, retail giants should also look at the possibilities of tapping rural entrepreneurship.

Pricing Strategy, Distribution/Sales Force Plan and Promotion Strategy

Pricing Strategy

As the procurement of these good could be done locally within the district, thus transportation cost could come down. Thus for the common products of the SHGs and retailers, considering the transportation cost, lower pricing strategy could be adopted. As labelling, branding and maintaining consistent quality would involve some marginal cost, thus price per unit of the product would be higher than the SHG price and lower than the mall price. On the other hand pricing of the mall products in rural areas would remain same as in their show room.

Distribution/Sales Force Plan

Distribution and sales force plan need not be altered so far as our business plan is concerned. However, a district level procurement agency could be formed to collect the good from the SHGs. In Ganjam district, the district level federation of SHGs could be appointed in this regard with required training and exposure visits.

Promotion Strategy

At present we are witnessing such a time period, when all consumers are sufficiently aware of both the products.

If SHG products are sold in mall outlets, on the price front, the product would be cheaper. Only thing, if due quality is maintained in the SHG products, there is no reason on the part of the customers to disfavour those products. On the other hand, promoting mall products in rural areas would require display and demo use of the products.

Financials Around the Plan

Information regarding sales turnover and the percentage share of each item in the sales proceeds per day in the retail malls is confidential and not readily available with us. Thus, a detailed financial analysis and cost benefit analysis type of study couldn't be undertaken. However, if funds are made available from any suitable agency, such type of study could be taken up. But our study team is confident enough that the market synergy proposed herein could render much benefit to both the parties along with tremendous social benefits as outlined in our hypothetical discussion.

Micro-finance and its Role in India

Dr. Ramakrushna Mahapatra*
Sunita Patra**

Introduction

In India, despite the economic growth at national level at 9.4 per cent in 2006-07 it has declined to around 6 per cent in 2008-09,[1] poverty remains a serious problem for policymakers because the growth is mainly driven by growth in a few sectors in urban areas, such as industry and service sectors.[2] Incidence of poverty in India is estimated by the quintessential large sample surveys on household consumer expenditure and according to the Uniform Recall Period (URP) consumption distribution data in 2004-05, rural areas yields a poverty ratio of 28.3 per cent, 25.7 per cent in urban areas and 27.5 per cent for the country as a whole (Government of India, 2009). Although the proportion of persons below the poverty line (BPL) has declined from

* **Senior Faculty Member of Commerce, Gaeddug College of Business Studies, RUB, RGoB, Chukhha, E-mail: drmp12@gmail.com**

** **Faculty Member, Presidency College, BAM,** *E-mail:* **suni.patra4@gmail.com**

around 36 per cent of the population in 1993-94 to 28 per cent in 2004-05, the poverty reduction still remains the country's major challenge in the 21st century.

Until the early 1990s, the financial services were provided through a variety of State-sponsored institutions, which resulted in impressive achievements in expanding access to credit particularly among the rural poor (Arun and Mosley, 2003). Although many of these commercial bank branches in rural areas wer unprofitable, they did play a positive role in financial savings and reducing poverty which is evident in the fact during the period 1951-1991 the share of total financial institutions in rural household debt has increased from 8.8 per cent to 53.3 per cent and the role of moneylenders has declined significantly during this period (Arun and Mosley, 2003; Basu and Srivastava 2005). However, despite the vast network of banking and cooperative finance institutions and strong micro components in various programmes, the performance of formal financial sector is still far behind in reaching out to reflect and respond the requirements of the poor.

The term 'micro-finance' refers to small-scale financial service both credit and savings - that are extended to the poor in rural, semi-urban and urban areas. The poor need micro-finance to undertake economic activity, smoothen consumption, mitigate vulnerability to income shocks (in times of illness and natural disasters), increase savings and support self-empowerment. Micro-credit is the most common product offering. Micro-finance in India is synonymous with micro-credit; because savings, thrift and micro-insurance constitute a miniscule segment of the micro-finance space. In India, most micro-finance loans are in the range of Rs. 5,000 to Rs. 20,000 (the Development and Regulation Bill, 2007,[3] defines micro-finance loans as loans with amounts not exceeding Rs. 50,000 in aggregate per individual/small enterprise). CRISIL estimates that around 120 million households in India continue to face financial exclusion. This translates into a credit demand of around Rs. 1.2 trillion.[4] The MFIs are the main players in the micro-finance space in India, their primary product is micro-credit. Other players that extend micro-finance services, in addition to their core business, include banks and insurance companies, agricultural and diary co-operatives, corporate organizations such as fertilizer companies and handloom houses and the postal network. Additionally there are specialized lenders, called apex MFIs that provide both loans and capacity building support to MFIs.[5]

The Differentiating Factors of MFIs

MFIs differ from one another in terms of:

1. Lending model;
2. Loan repayment structure;
3. Mode of interest rate calculation;
4. Product offerings; and
5. Legal structure.

In terms of lending model, MFIs may be classified as lenders to groups or as lenders to individuals. In India, MFIs usually adopt the group-based lending models, which are of two types - the Self-help Group (SHG) model and the Joint-Liability Group (JLG)/solidarity group model. Under the SHG model, an MFI lends to a group of 10 to 20 women. Under the SHG-bank linkage model, an NGO promotes a group and gets banks to extend loans to the group. Under the JLG model, loans are extended to and recovered from, each member of the group (unlike under the SHG model, where the loans is extended to the group as a whole). The most popular JLG models are the Grameen Bank model (developed by Grameen Bank, Bangladesh) and the ASA model (developed by ASA, a leading Bangladesh-based NGO-MFI). Most of the large MFIs in India follow a hybrid of the group models.

The model of lending to individuals is similar to the retail loan financing model of banks. In India, MFIs adopting the group-lending models extend individual loans to more successful borrowers who have completed a few loans cycles as part of a group (who have relatively large credit requirements and good repayment bank record). Corporates and co-operatives typically diary firms and sugar mills are also known to undertake microfinance by extending credit to farmers, this helps the companies strengthen their procurement and distribution networks.

The MFIs are also differentiated on the basis of their loan repayment structures. Most MFIs following the JLG model adopt the weekly and fortnightly repayment structure. Those under the SHG model have a monthly repayment structure. The MFIs lending to traders in market places also offer daily repayment, while MFIs extending agricultural loans have bullet and cash-flow based repayment structures depending on the crop patterns.MFIs following the JLG model charge flat interest rates of 12 to 18% on their loans, while The MFIs following the SHG model charge 18 to 24 per cent interest per annum based on the reducing balancing method. In addition to interest rates, some MFIs also charge a processing fee comprising a certain proportion of the loan amount sanctioned at the time of disbursement.

Most MFIs in India are solely engaged in extending micro-credit, a few also extend saving, thrift, insurance, pension and remittance facilities. For providing insurance facilities, MFIs have tied up with insurance companies and mutual networks (funds created by community-owned organizations), some MFIs also do underwriting on their own.

The MFIs offer savings services in two ways - the savings are either collected by the MFIs on the SHG. In the later method, the MFIs or NGOs encourage the SHG to collect savings/thrift from each member of the group on a weekly/monthly basis and rotate the savings/thrift among members. An MFI collecting savings from borrowers may either make it compulsory for borrowers/members to have savings with it, or offer voluntary savings services to both members/non-members. Only MFIs registered as cooperatives or depositing NBFCs can collect savings/ deposits, a few MFIs registered as societies and trusts continue to accept saving/deposits, and thus face regulatory risks (for more details, refer section on absence of regulatory control).

By taking into account legal structures, MFIs may be classified as follows:

Not for Profit MFIs

- Societies (e.g. such as Bandhan, Rashtriya Seva Samithi and Gram Utthan.)
- Public trusts (such as Shri Khetra Dharmasthala Rural Development Project, and community development centre.)
- Non-profit companies (such as Indian association for savings and credit, and cash per micro-credit)

Mutual Benefit MFIs

- Co-operatives registered under State or national acts (such as Pustikar Lagh Vyaparik Pratisthan Bachat and Sakh Sahkari Samiti Limited)
- Mutually-aided co-operative societies (MACS, such as Sewa Mutually Aided Co-operative Thrift Societies Federation Ltd.)

For Profit MFIs

- Non-banking financial companies (NBFCs, such as Bharatiya Samruddhi Finance Ltd, Share Microfin Ltd, SKS Microfinance Ltd and Spandan Sphoorthy Finance Ltd.)

- Producer Companies (such as Sri Vijaya Visakha Milk Producers Co. Ltd).
- Local area banks (the only such MFI is Krishna Bhima Samruddhi Local Area Bank.)

Growth of MFIs in India

The micro-finance market in India is expected to grow rapidly, supported by the Government of India's initiatives to achieve greater financial inclusion, and growth in the country's retail sector. The MFIs have a grassroot level reach and understanding of the economic needs of the poor. The growing retail market in India provides opportunities for MFIs to act as intermediaries in the retail supply chain. The banking sector will also help the micro-finance sector grow. Banks are expected to use MFIs to meet their financial inclusion targets by allowing MFIs to open bank accounts, and distribute financial services and other structured products.

The micro-finance sector has passed its revolutionary phase, when the profit-oriented working model of MFIs was perceived by the market as exceptionable. Also investors now have wider choice of MFIs with scalable process. NGO-MFIs have been acquiring dormant NBFC for regulatory financial and operational reasons. Many large players are now focused on urban micro-finance and have begun extending loans to individuals.

The micro-finance sector and MFIs in India are estimated to have outstanding total loans of Rs. 160 to Rs. 175 billion and Rs. 110 to Rs. 120 billion respectively, as on 31st March, 2001. The micro-finance sector in India is fragmented, there are more than 3000 MFIs, NGOs and NGO-MFIs, of which about 400 have active lending programmes. The top MFIs are estimated to account for around 74 per cent of the total loans outstanding for MFIs, around 17 MFIs had outstanding loans of more than rupees one billion as on 31st March, 2009 with the top three MFIs crossing Rs. 10 billion in terms of outstanding loan portfolios on that date. The outstanding loans of MFIs have increased to Rs. 114 billion as on 31st March, 2009 from Rs. 60 billion a year ago Table 12.1. The growth in disbursements by MFIs was more than that of the SHG-bank linkage programme during 2007-08. MFIs disbursements have increased aggressively at a compound annual growth rate (CAGR) of 90 per cent, over the past four years. CRISIL estimates the overall disbursements during 2008-09 to be around Rs. 287 billion of which disbursements of Rs. 185 billion were made by MFIs (Refer Table 12.2). This is resultant ability to attract capital and resources during the past two years.

Table 12.1: Growth Trends of Loans Outstanding and Borrowers

Year	Loans Outstanding (Rs. in billion)	Borrowers (No. in million)
March 2006	16	3
March 2007	32	5
March 2008	60	9
March 2009	114	16

Source: Industry, NABARD.

Table 12.2: Trend in Disbursements (Rs. in billion)

Year	MFIs	SHG-Bank linkage	Total
2004-05	15	30	45
2005-06	27	45	72
2006-07	44	66	110
2007-08	95	88	183
2008-09	185	102	287

Source: Industry, NABARD.

A majority of MFIs, including the larger players, operated mainly in South India till 2005-06. Since, 2006-07, however the large MFIs have extended their presence to States such as Maharashtra, Chandigarh, Orissa, Jharkhand and West Bengal. Over the past two years, the growth of the micro-finance sector in eastern India was driven primarily by capacity enhancement initiatives by the apex MFIs, and tapping of growth opportunities in the eastern market by South India based MFIs and banks. Many of the large MFIs, nevertheless continue to have a significant exposure to south India.

Improving Earning Profile

Improvement in lending rates, in branch and employee productivity, and increasing efficiencies on account of growth in loan portfolios have helped MFIs of all categories enhance their operating self-sufficiency (OSS)[6] ratios. The CRISIL believes that MFIs OSS ratios will increase over the medium term; this is because MFIs (particularly the large ones) have increased their lending rates, with several players also charging upfront processing fees.

Heavy Dependence on Banks and Financial Institutions (FIs)

The MFIs are dependant on borrowings from banks and FIs, and do not raise debt from the capital market. Thus, large NBFC-MFIs face higher cost of borrowing than most large retail finance NBFCs in the country. Banks categorize their lending to MFIs as priority sector advance, which has helped MFIs raise timely resources. However, for many MFIs funding sources are restricted to private banks and apex MFIs. The public sector banks have not been aggressive lenders to MFIs. The large and Mid-sized MFIs and NBFC-MFIs primarily borrow from private and foreign banks, while the smaller MFIs borrow mainly from private banks and apex lenders.

The lending model plays a key role in determining a MFIs borrowing profile. Public sector banks (PSBs) with their wide-spread branch networks; prefer lending directly through the SHG-bank linkage route. Moreover, PSBs prefer to lend to those MFIs that have adopted the SHG model. The PSBs accounted for 36 per cent of total borrowings of societies and trusts (refer Table 12.3) as against only 10 per cent of MFI following the JLG model, as on 31st March, 2008. Thus NGO-MFIs (societies and trust) have better access to funds from PSBs than MFIs that are companies.

Table 12.3: Borrowing Profile (Based on Lending Model)

	SHG	JLG	Diversified
PSBs	36%	10%	8%
Private Banks	30%	35%	34%
Foreign Banks	10%	30%	28%
Apex MFIs	20%	19%	20%
Others	4%	6%	10%
Total	**100%**	**100%**	**100%**

Source: Industry, NABARD.

However, this scenario of PSBs lending predominantly to SHG model based MFIs seems poised for change, with the large NBFCs continuing to aggressively target PSBs to meet their credit demands.

Absence of Regulatory Control

Micro-finance activities are undertaken by organizations that are registered under sectoral legal forms. However, currently, only NBFCs are under the regulatory and supervisory purview-the NBFCs are regulated by RBI. The absence of prudential norms and accounting guidelines for non-NBFC MFI leads to lack of uniformity in accounting practices and highly-leveraged balance sheets among MFIs.

The financial statements of the micro-finance programmes of most non-NBFC MFIs do not provide the true financial picture. There was a proposal by Government of India to bring in legislation in 2006 to regulate the entire micro-finance sector in India, the regulation, however is yet to be materialized.

Savings is an important component of micro-finance. Currently however, savings and deposit services can be offered only by banks and cooperatives. The NBFCs can raise deposits only after obtaining a license from RBI and meeting norms (such as having an investment grade credit rating).The Trusts and societies (un incorporated bodies) cannot accept savings/deposits as per Section 455 of the RBI Act, 1934.

A few NGO-MFIs and non-NGO-MFIs continue to offer in-house insurance facilities by underwriting on their own, although this is a clear violation of insurance regulations.

Political Sensitivity of Interest Rates

In April ,1999,[7] Reserve Bank of India issued a circular allowing MFIs to fix interest rates on the loans they extend. However, interest rates charged to the poor constitute a politically-sensitive issue, and therefore, a challenging proposition for MFIs. Although acts pertaining to money-lending and loans in the States specify interest rate ceilings, these are applicable largely to societies and trusts. Over the past years, MFIs especially in Andhra Pradesh, Tamil Nadu, and Karnataka, have often been targeted by local district administrations.

Given MFIs operating and cost structures, most MFIs need to charge high interest rates to recover costs and remain in business. Sadhan, the industry association has suggested a voluntary mutually code of conduct under which MFIs provide information regarding interest rates and other charges to clients. Though many MFIs highlight only the flat interest rates and processing fees, a few MFIs did mention the effective interest rates in their borrowers' passbooks as on 31st March, 2009.

Pressure on Process and Controls Due to Aggressive Growth Plans

The MFIs risk management practices have weakened over the past couple of years, on account of a shift in focus towards business growth and network expansion. Some credit sanction and monitoring practices have been diluted. These include lending to clients with multiple loans from different MFIs, reduction in the average waiting period for loans, and doing away with staggered disbursements to JLGs and loan utilization checks post disbursement. Rapid expansions to new geographies have also put pressure on the internal control mechanisms and audit function, as these have not received adequate focus in the past two years.

Nevertheless, there has been some improvement in MFIs' operations, this includes installation of software for monitoring loans, upgrade in cash management services, and availability of banking facilities to MFIs operating in rural and semi-urban areas. Many small and mid-sized MFIs have also benefited from the technical support, such as documentation of internal policies and process mapping, with capacity-building support, particularly from apex MFIs.

Weak in Governance of MFIs

The legal structure and the attendant regulatory requirements of an MFI have a strong bearing on governance practices because they influence management practices and levels of transparency. All legal structures other than the formal company structure, suffer for want of adequate regulations and disclosure standards. This also creates a virtuous/vicious cycle phenomenon such as; MFIs that have the willingness and minimum capital funds to embrace a corporate structure as an NBFC attract outside investors more easily, which in turn fosters better governance and disclosure standards. In contrast, MFIs that are either unable (for lack of adequate sponsor funding) or unwilling to convert to a corporate structures tend to remain "Closed" to transparency and improved governance standards, and therefore, continue to be unable to attract capital. Moreover, some MFIs particularly, NGO-MFIs, continue to face challenges in striking a balance between their social and business goals, two seemingly conflicting objectives. This often results in poor internal control systems, lack of accountability, and suboptimal performance.

The micro-finance has acquired in India as an economically viable (even moderately, profitable, scalable and sustainable) lending activity, applies only to a few MFIs that are typically structured as NBFCs with notable participation from international private equity funds. Many MFIs are new and have begun operations on a relatively clean state, focusing on establishing a strong board, and internal control systems.

With donor and grant funds drying up and related voluntary services dwindling, micro-finance has become a key activity for several NGO-MFIs in India. However, their managements have not adapted and equipped themselves adequately to manage this evolution, with the result that governance, disclosure and accountability have suffered in many cases. Unless NGO-MFIs restructure their boards and management to drive a reasonable commercial orientation into their operating philosophy and mission, the attendant benefits of good internal control systems and transparency are unlikely to materialize. This will ultimately hinder the sustainability of their operations.

Conclusion

Funding (both equity and debt) will not be a constraint for the large players in India's microfinance sector. The average ratio is expected to remain adequate for the larger NBFCs-MFIs (which are regulated) as most of these entities are able to raise capital. Most mid-sized MFIs are in a process of charging their legal structure. The overall asset quality of MFIs is healthy however; this is expected to decline marginally. The key factors that can drive success for MFIs are robust systems, and processes and efficiency and productivity levels, maintaining asset quality, prevention of credit losses and capital erosion and remaining adequately capitalized to fund growth plans.

NOTES

1. Govt. of India, Fact Sheet, 2009.
2. The average annual output growth rates in industry and services sectors in the period 1994-2004 and 5.6% and 8.2% respectively, while that in agricultural sector is 2.0% (based on World Bank Data in 2005 taken from http://dev data.worldbank.org/AAG/ind aag.pdf). The poverty head count ratio has been much higher in rural areas than in urban areas (e.g. Deaton and Kozel 2005 and Sen and Himanshu 2004).
3. The bill, which envisages the regulation of the micro-finance sector is under the Parliament consideration.
4. The number of households facing exclusion has been arrived at by adding rural households facing financial exclusion (93 million) and urban below poverty line (BPL) households (18 million). The average credit demand per household has been estimated at Rs. 10,000 per annum.
5. National Bank for Agriculture and Rural Development, Small Industries Development Bank of India, Rastriya Mahila Kosha and Friends of Women's World Banking are the apex MFIs in India.
6. Defined as ratio of total income to total expense. It does not include revenue grants received and expenses out of revenue grants.
7. Reserve Bank of India, Circular RPCD, No. PLBC. 94/04.09.01/ 98-99, dated, April 24, 1999.

REFERENCES

Arun, T. and Hulme, D. (2003), Balancing Supply and Demand: The Emerging Agenda for Micro-finance Institutions, *Journal of Micro-finance*, 5(2), 1-5.

Basu, P. and Srivastava, P. (2005), "Scaling-up Micro-finance for India's Rural Poor", *Policy Research Working Paper 3646*, World Bank: Washington.

Deaton, A. and Kozel, K. (2005), "Data and Dogma: The Great Indian Poverty Debate," *World Bank Research Observer*, 20(2), 177-199.

Mosley, P., and Arun, T. (2003), "Improving Access to Rural Finance in India: Supply Side Constraints," Unpublished Background Paper to the Economic and Sector Work Study on Access to Finance, World Bank, South Asia Finance and Private Sector Development Unit.

NABARD, Mumbai, 2009.

Sen, A. and Himanshu (2004), "Poverty and Inequality in India-II: Widening Disparities during the 1990s", *Economic and Political Weekly*, September 25, 4361-4376.

Index

N

O